Marian Cox & Robert Swan

The Poetry of Carol Ann Duffy

Selected Poems · The World's Wife

D1079760

THE HENLEY COLLEGE LIBRARY

Philip Allan Updates, part of the Hodder Education Group, an Hachette Livre UK company, Market Place, Deddington, Oxfordshire OX15 0SE

Orders
Bookpoint Ltd, 130 Milton Park, Abingdon, Oxfordshire, OX14 4SB
tel: 01235 827720
fax: 01235 400454
e-mail: uk.orders@bookpoint.co.uk
Lines are open 9.00 a.m.–5.00 p.m., Monday to Saturday, with a 24-hour message answering service. You can also order through the Philip Allan Updates website: www.philipallan.co.uk

© Philip Allan Updates 2005

ISBN 978-1-84489-210-5

All rights reserved; no part of this publication may be reproduced, stored in a retrieval system, or transmitted, in any form or by any means, electronic, mechanical, photocopying, recording or otherwise without either the prior written permission of Philip Allan Updates or a licence permitting restricted copying in the United Kingdom issued by the Copyright Licensing Agency Ltd, Saffron House, 6–10 Kirby Street, London EC1N 8TS.

In all cases we have attempted to trace and credit copyright owners of material used.

Printed in Malta

Philip Allan Updates' policy is to use papers that are natural, renewable and recyclable products and made from wood grown in sustainable forests. The logging and manufacturing processes are expected to conform to the environmental regulations of the country of origin.

Contents

Introduction

Aims of the guide

The purpose of this Student Text Guide to the poetry of Carol Ann Duffy is to enable you to organise your thoughts and responses to the poems, to deepen your understanding of key features and aspects, and finally to help you to address the particular requirements of examination questions in order to obtain the best possible grade.

This guide includes information applicable to the poetry of Carol Ann Duffy in general, and it has separate sections on the poems in the collections of *Selected Poems* and *The World's Wife*. Because some of the poems from the latter collection are also included *Selected Poems*, students need to check carefully which poems are set by their examination board and read the appropriate sections of this guide. The poems are dealt with in the order in which they appear in the respective set editions.

It is assumed that you have read and studied the poems already under the guidance of a teacher or lecturer. This is a revision guide, not an introduction, although some of its content serves the purpose of providing initial background. It can be read in its entirety in one sitting, or it can be dipped into and used as a reference guide to specific and separate aspects of the poetry.

The remainder of this Introduction outlines the Assessment Objectives, with a summary of the requirements of the various examination boards and their schemes of assessment; a revision scheme which gives a suggested programme for using the material in the guide; and extensive practical advice on writing essay answers.

The Text Guidance section consists of a series of subsections which examine key aspects of the poetry including contexts, interpretations and controversies, and notes on the poems. Emboldened terms within the Text Guidance section are glossed in 'literary terms and concepts' on pp. 90–94.

The final section, Questions and Answers, includes examples of essay questions of different types with mark schemes, exemplar essay plans and samples of marked work.

Assessment Objectives

The Assessment Objectives (AOs) for A-level English Literature are common to all boards:

AO1	communicate clearly the knowledge, understanding and insight appropriate to literary study, using appropriate terminology and accurate and coherent written expression

AO2i	respond with knowledge and understanding to literary texts of different types and periods
AO2ii	respond with knowledge and understanding to literary texts of different types and periods, exploring and commenting on relationships and comparisons between literary texts
AO3	show detailed understanding of the ways in which writers' choices of form, structure and language shape meanings
AO4	articulate independent opinions and judgements, informed by different interpretations of literary texts by other readers
AO5i	show understanding of the contexts in which literary texts are written and understood
AO5ii	evaluate the significance of cultural, historical and other contextual influences on literary texts and study

A summary of each Assessment Objective is given below and would be worth memorising:

AO1	clarity of written communication
AO2	informed personal response in relation to time and genre (literary context)
AO3	the creative literary process (context of writing)
AO4	critical and interpretative response (context of reading)
AO5	evaluation of influences (cultural context)

It is essential that you pay close attention to the AOs and their weighting, for the board for which you are entered. These are what the examiner will be looking for, and you must address them *directly* and *specifically*, in addition to proving general familiarity with and understanding of the text, and being able to present an argument clearly, relevantly and convincingly.

Remember that the examiners are seeking above all else evidence of an *informed personal response* to the text. A revision guide such as this can help you to understand the text and to form your own opinions, but it cannot replace your own ideas and responses as an individual reader.

Revision advice

For the examined units it is possible that either brief or more extensive revision will be necessary because the original study of the text took place some time previously.

It is therefore useful to know how to go about revising and which tried and tested methods are considered the most successful for literature exams at all levels, from GCSE to degree finals.

Below is a guide on how not to do it — think of reasons why not in each case. **Don't**:

- leave it until the last minute
- assume you remember the text well enough and don't need to revise at all
- spend hours designing a beautiful revision schedule
- revise more than one text at the same time
- think you don't need to revise because it is an open book exam
- decide in advance what you think the questions will be and revise only for those
- try to memorise particular essay plans
- reread texts randomly and aimlessly
- revise for longer than 2 hours in one sitting
- miss school lessons in order to work alone at home
- try to learn a whole ring-binder's worth of work
- rely on a study guide instead of the text

There are no short-cuts to effective exam revision; the only one way to know a text well, and to know your way around it in an exam, is to have done the necessary studying. If you use the following method, in six easy stages, for both open and closed book revision, you will not only revisit and reassess all your previous work on the text in a manageable way but will be able to distil, organise and retain your knowledge. Don't try to do it all in one go: take regular breaks for refreshment and a change of scene.

(1) Between a month and a fortnight before the exam, depending on your schedule (a simple list of stages with dates displayed in your room, not a work of art!), you will need to reread the text, this time taking stock of all the underlinings and marginal annotations as well. As you read, collect onto sheets of A4 the essential ideas and quotations as you come across them. The acts of selecting key material and recording it as notes are natural ways of stimulating thought and aiding memory.

(2) Reread the highlighted areas and marginal annotations in your critical extracts and background handouts, and add anything useful from them to your list of notes and quotations. Then reread your previous essays and the teacher's comments. As you look back through essays written earlier in the course, you should have the pleasant sensation of realising that you can now write much better on the text than you could then. You will also discover that much of your huge file of notes is redundant or repeated, and that you have changed your mind about some beliefs, so that the distillation process is not too daunting. Selecting what is important is the way to crystallise your knowledge and understanding.

(3) During the run-up to the exam you need to do lots of practice essay plans to help you identify any gaps in your knowledge and give you practice in planning in 5–8 minutes. Past paper titles for you to plan are provided in this guide, some of which can be done as full timed essays — and marked strictly according to exam criteria — which will show whether length and timing are problematic for you. If you have not seen a copy of a real exam paper before you take your first module, ask to see a past paper so that you are familiar with the layout and rubric.

(4) About a week before the exam, reduce your two or three sides of A4 notes to a double-sided postcard of very small, dense writing. Collect a group of keywords by once again selecting and condensing, and use abbreviations for quotations (first and last word), and character and place names (initials). The act of choosing and writing out the short quotations will help you to focus on the essential issues, and to recall them quickly in the exam. Make sure that your selection covers the main themes and includes examples of symbolism, style, comments on character, examples of irony, point of view or other significant aspects of the text. Previous class discussion and essay writing will have indicated which quotations are useful for almost any title; pick those which can serve more than one purpose, for instance those which reveal character and theme, and are also an example of language. In this way a minimum number of quotations can have maximum application.

(5) You now have in a compact, accessible form all the material for any possible essay title. There are only half a dozen themes relevant to a literary text so if you have covered these, you should not meet with any nasty surprises when you read the exam questions. You don't need to refer to your file of paperwork again, or even to the text. For the few days before the exam, you can read through your handy postcard whenever and wherever you get the opportunity. Each time you read it, which will only take a few minutes, you are reminding yourself of all the information you will be able to recall in the exam to adapt to the general title or to support an analysis of particular passages.

(6) A fresh, active mind works wonders, and information needs time to settle, so don't try to cram just before the exam. Relax the night before and get a good night's sleep. Then you will be able to enter the exam room with all the confidence of a well-prepared candidate.

Writing examination essays

Essay content

One of the key skills you are being asked to demonstrate at A-level is the ability to select and tailor your knowledge of the text and its background to the question

set in the exam paper. In order to reach the highest levels, you need to avoid 'pre-packaged' essays which lack focus, relevance and coherence, and which simply contain everything you know about the text. Be ruthless in rejecting irrelevant material, after considering whether it can be made relevant by a change of emphasis. Aim to cover the whole question, not just part of it; your response needs to demonstrate breadth and depth, covering the full range of text elements: character, event, theme and language. Only half a dozen approaches are possible for any set text, though they may be phrased in a variety of ways, and they are likely to refer to the key themes of the text. Preparation of the text therefore involves extensive discussion and practice at manipulating these core themes so that there should be no surprises in the exam. An apparently new angle is more likely to be something familiar presented in an unfamiliar way and you should not panic or reject the choice of question because you think you know nothing about it.

Exam titles are open-ended in the sense that there is not an obvious right answer, and you would therefore be unwise to give a dismissive, extreme or entirely one-sided response. The question would not have been set if the answer were not debatable. An ability and willingness to see both sides is an Assessment Objective and shows independence of judgement as a reader. Don't be afraid to explore the issues and don't try to tie the text into one neat interpretation. If there is ambiguity, it is likely to be deliberate on the part of the author and must be discussed; literary texts are complex and often paradoxical, and it would be a misreading of them to suggest that there is only one possible interpretation. You are not expected, however, to argue equally strongly or extensively for both sides of an argument, since personal opinion is an important factor. It is advisable to deal with the alternative view at the beginning of your response, and then construct your own view as the main part of the essay. This makes it less likely that you will appear to cancel out your own line of argument.

Choosing the right question

The first skill you must show when presented with the exam paper is the ability to choose the better, for you, of the two questions on your text where there is a choice. This is not to say that you should always go for the same type of essay (whole-text or poem-based), and if the question is not one with which you feel happy for any reason, you should seriously consider the other, even if it is not the type you normally prefer. It is unlikely but possible that a question contains a word you are not sure you know the meaning of, in which case it would be safer to choose the other one.

Don't be tempted to choose a question because of its similarity to one you have already done. Freshness and thinking on the spot usually produce a better result than attempted recall of a previous essay which may have received only a mediocre mark in the first place. The exam question is unlikely to have exactly the same focus and your response may seem 'off centre' as a result, as well as stale and perfunctory in expression. Essay questions fall into the following categories: close section analysis and relation to whole text; characterisation; setting and atmosphere; structure and effectiveness; genre; language and style; themes and issues. Remember, however, that themes are relevant to all essays and that analysis, not just description, is always required.

Once you have decided which exam question to attempt, follow the procedure below for whole-text and passage-based, open- and closed-book essays.

(1) Underline all the key words in the question and note how many parts the question has.

(2) Plan your answer, using aspects of the key words and parts of the question as sub-headings, in addition to themes. Aim for 10–12 ideas. Check that the Assessment Objectives are covered.

(3) Support your argument by selecting the best examples of characters, events, imagery and quotations to prove your points. Remove ideas for which you can find no evidence.

(4) Structure your answer by grouping and numbering your points in a logical progression. Identify the best general point to keep for the conclusion.

(5) Introduce your essay with a short paragraph setting the context and defining the key words in the question as broadly, but relevantly, as possible.

(6) Write the rest of the essay, following your structured plan but adding extra material if it occurs to you. Paragraph your writing and consider expression, especially sentence structure and vocabulary choices, as you write. Signal changes in the direction of your argument with paragraph openers such as 'Furthermore' and 'However'. Use plenty of short, integrated quotations and use the words of the text rather than your own where possible. Use technical terms appropriately, and write concisely and precisely, avoiding vagueness and ambiguity.

(7) Your conclusion should sound conclusive and make it clear that you have answered the question. It should be an overview of the question and the text, not a repetition or a summary of points already made.

(8) Cross out your plan with a neat, diagonal line.

(9) Check your essay for content, style, clarity and accuracy. With neat crossings-out, correct errors of fact, spelling, grammar and punctuation. Improve expression if possible, and remove any repetition and irrelevance. Add clarification and missing evidence, if necessary, using omission marks or asterisks. Even at this stage, good new material can be added.

There is no such thing as a perfect or model essay; flawed essays can gain full marks. There is always something more which could have been said, and examiners realise that students have limitations when writing under pressure in timed conditions. You are not penalised for what you didn't say in comparison to some idealised concept of the answer, but rewarded for the knowledge and understanding you have shown. It is not as difficult as you may think to do well, provided that you are familiar with the text and have sufficient essay-writing experience. If you follow the above process and **underline, plan**, **support**, **structure**, **write** and **check**, you can't go far wrong.

Text Guidance

Contexts

Life and works

Carol Ann Duffy was born on 23 December 1955 in Glasgow, Scotland, the daughter of Frank Duffy and Mary Black. Mary was Irish, as were Frank's grandparents, so Duffy is three-quarters Irish, born in Scotland and brought up predominantly in England, which may go some way to explaining her concern with identity.

Frank Duffy was an electrical fitter and lifelong Labour Party supporter; he stood unsuccessfully as a Labour Party candidate in the 1983 general election. When Carol Ann was 6 years old the family moved to Stafford in northwest England, where she was to spend the remainder of her childhood, attending a succession of local schools and ending up at Stafford High School for Girls. It is a reasonable assumption that much of her concern with childhood alienation derives from the experience of being uprooted and moved to a culture in which, with her Glasgow accent and urban background, she would have been seen, and no doubt treated, as an outsider.

Carol Ann was precocious in a number of ways. She sent her first collection of poems to a publisher when she was 15, and from the age of 16 she was having an affair with the celebrated poet Adrian Henri, who was 39 at the time. This lasted for several years, and led her to go to Liverpool University in 1974 in order to be near him. She studied philosophy and graduated in 1977.

Duffy worked in a variety of fields while she attempted to establish herself as a writer. Her first collection of poems, *Standing Female Nude*, was published in 1985, and she was then able to turn to writing full time. Despite her early liaison with Henri, she has for many years lived with a female partner, the poet Jackie Kay. Duffy has a daughter, born in 1995, but the father has not been involved in her upbringing.

Since 1996 Duffy has lectured at Manchester Metropolitan University. She rose to prominence in the media in 1999, when she was suggested as a possible candidate for the position of poet laureate following the death of Ted Hughes. It is not clear whether she would have accepted such a position in the establishment, and in any case Andrew Motion was eventually appointed after much discussion in the media as to the suitability for the post of a 'lesbian unmarried mother', as she was described.

In addition to her collections of poems for adults, Duffy has written two plays, two collections of poems for children, and has edited a number of other volumes of poetry.

Poetry collections for adults

Standing Female Nude (1985)

This was Duffy's first published collection of poetry for adults. Its title is taken from one of the poems based upon a work of art ('Oppenheim's Cup and Saucer' is another) and includes a number of political and 'issue' poems.

Selling Manhattan (1987)

The collection title is again taken from a keynote poem. Pursuing similar **themes** to *Standing Female Nude*, this collection is perhaps best known for hard-hitting poems such as 'Psychopath'.

The Other Country (1990)

This is Duffy's first collection for which the title is an **ironic** reference in its own right, rather than simply being the title of one of the constituent poems. It **alludes** to the celebrated quotation from L. P. Hartley's *The Go-Between*: 'The past is another country. They do things differently there.' The phrase 'another country' was also the title of a widely-seen film about public school spies in Britain in the 1930s and 1940s. Duffy's choice of title therefore economically calls to the reader's attention two of her recurring themes: alienation and translocation, both literally and **metaphorically**, and the past.

Mean Time (1993)

Continuing the trend set by *The Other Country*, *Mean Time* is a resonant and thought-provoking title. It suggests at least three distinct interpretations: 'in the meantime', i.e. events happening while others are continuing, in the background or elsewhere; that time is itself mean, because of the awareness of what it takes away and will not give back; and, perhaps more distantly, the question of the meaning of time — what does time mean? — and how the poet is to respond to such a question. It is also perhaps an echo of Greenwich Mean Time, the universal measure of time, which hints that the themes of the poems have a universal relevance.

The World's Wife (1999)

There is great subtlety in Duffy's choice of title. Its primary reference is an echo of the familiar phrase, 'the world and his wife', meaning everybody. This is doubly offensive to a feminist such as Duffy: first, the suggestion is that only men matter, and constitute the world; second, it implies that women have a purpose and a role only as the appendages and property of men. The aim of this collection is not merely to challenge these assumptions, but to turn them on their head. This is most succinctly done in 'Mrs Darwin': far from being an adjunct, Darwin's wife, Duffy is suggesting, may actually have had the idea which was to make *him* famous. Using the wives (or, in some cases, female counterparts) of celebrated men as a structure is ironic and mischievous, and allows Duffy to write some of her most stinging and overtly feminist poetry.

Feminine Gospels (2002)

This is Duffy's most recent collection of poetry for adults. It returns to the subjects and **styles** of her earlier work, except that, in keeping with the title, all the poems have female voices. One poem, 'The Laughter of Stafford Girls' High', is very long (it makes up a third of the entire collection) and brings her back, again, to her schooldays. In the concluding poem, 'Death and the Moon', she revealingly suggests that 'poems are prayers'.

The 1960s

The 1960s was a significant decade in British history. The period of 'austerity' which began during the Second World War did not end until the early 1950s (rationing of food and other items continued until 1954). During the late 1950s a number of changes occurred: pop music, explicitly aimed at teenagers, began to emerge; film became an important influence on young people; televisions and telephones were installed in many British homes. Together, these led to the revolution of mass media and mass communications.

Postcolonial Britain

Britain was a major imperial power until the Second World War: the British empire was the largest in the world and spanned the globe. After the war it became clear that the era of empire was over, and the granting of independence to India, Pakistan and Ceylon as early as 1947 was a precursor to the process of wholesale decolonisation which began in the late 1950s. This led to two significant changes in British society. The first was the mass immigration of non-European people from former colonies that, in time, turned Britain into a multiracial society. This was controversial; racism became an important part of British life, and was whipped up by right-wing nationalist political leaders. The second change was more subtle: from being a major world power, Britain slowly became a small country in Europe, and many people had difficulty in coming to terms with Britain's loss of importance and influence on the world stage.

Politics and culture

Britain had been a democracy since the nineteenth century, but a combination of factors led to the right-wing Conservative Party dominating British politics for much of the twentieth century. Conservatism is based on pragmatism, maintaining the traditional institutions of society, free enterprise and law and order. The left-wing Labour Party (not really socialist, but concerned with the rights of ordinary people) came to power in 1964, after 13 years of Conservative rule, and the new government seemed to usher in a period of renewed intellectual and cultural life in the country. It was the era of The Beatles, the most successful pop group ever, of 'Swinging Britain', with its outrageous fashion and personal liberation. The widespread introduction of the contraceptive pill meant that women could have sex without fear of the consequences, and by the end of the 1960s the 'sexual revolution' had swept away centuries of taboos — the poet Philip Larkin wrote that 'Sexual intercourse began/in nineteen sixty three' ('Annus Mirabilis', 1974). 'Free love' became popular and male homosexuality became legal for the first time. The hippy movement of the late 1960s seemed to promise an alternative lifestyle that was unconventional, anti-materialist and free-thinking. All these changes broke the stranglehold of conventional morality and class stereotyping that for some had made life in the 1950s and early 1960s stifling (see 'Litany').

Education

A significant contribution to these changes came with the introduction of compre-hensive schools by the Labour government. Since 1944, British state schools had been divided into grammar schools (see 'The Captain of the 1964 *Top of the Form* Team'), which gave an academic education to those children, predominantly middle class, who passed the '11-plus' examination, and secondary modern schools, which prepared children who failed, predominantly from the working class, for lives as unqualified workers. The new comprehensive schools would educate all children together (see 'Comprehensive'), and aimed to end the socio-educational divide. They were hailed as a great piece of social engineering that would finally remove the class divisions from British society. Although this goal was not achieved, compre-hensive schools did offer a serious academic education to any child who chose to take advantage of the opportunities on offer. 'Education for Leisure' is a wry comment on the aspiration that all workers in the future would enjoy increased leisure time and needed to be educated to use that time constructively.

Social change

The many social changes of the 1960s affected young people and women in particular. This was the era of pop art, mini-skirts, beat music, long hair and hallu-cinogenic drugs. Many young people went to pop festivals and love-ins, and joined the peace movement (which grew out of the Campaign for Nuclear Disarmament).

The feminist movement began to challenge the limitations placed upon women, and there was a feeling among educated young women that everything was possible. Grammar schools offered a route to university for lower middle-class women who would previously never have considered going to university, such as Margaret Thatcher, who became prime minister. The development of labour-saving domestic appliances, such as washing machines, liberated women from domestic drudgery; the introduction of synthetic materials, such as nylon, reduced the burden of doing the laundry and made cheap and brightly coloured clothes available. Increasingly,

women challenged the traditional view that their place was in the home and chose to make careers for themselves.

The sexual revolution meant that women were able to take the initiative in affairs of the heart once they were in control of their fertility. For the generation of Carol Ann Duffy, growing up during the 1960s, there seemed to be no limit to what might be achieved if women worked together, kept their nerve and tackled the discrimination that faced them, especially in the workplace.

Thatcherism

For most of the twentieth century, British politics was characterised by consensus — a broad agreement between the main parties on the general principles of policy. The two main parties, Labour and Conservative, were moderate; they agreed that there should be a mixed economy, with the state controlling key utilities but with the majority of companies in private hands. After the philanthropic legislation of the nineteenth century, there was general agreement that the state should take responsibility for key aspects of the lives of its citizens, including education, pensions, social security and, after 1947, healthcare. There was a periodic alternation of government between these two parties, but a change of government generally did not lead to dramatic changes in the way people lived.

One important exception to this pattern was the Labour government of Clement Attlee, which was elected in 1945 in the wake of the Second World War. It created the welfare state, of which the National Health Service was the most important component. This enjoyed support from both the major parties, however, and the Conservatives made no serious attempt to dismantle the welfare state when they returned to power in 1951.

The second exception was the period between 1979 and 1990 when Margaret Thatcher was prime minister. Thatcher, a grocer's daughter, became leader of the Conservative Party in 1975 and was elected as Britain's first woman prime minister in 1979. She had earlier won notoriety as 'Margaret Thatcher, Milk Snatcher' when, as education secretary, she ended the supply of free milk to schoolchildren. Feminists, however, had no expectation that their lot would improve: Thatcher was strongly anti-feminist — she refused to appoint any women to her cabinet, for example — and rejected the consensus which had underpinned British society for a century. She encouraged self-interest, especially in entrepreneurs such as Richard Branson, and in a celebrated statement said 'there is no such thing as society'. This was interpreted as absolving the wealthy from any social responsibility towards those less fortunate than themselves; in this she reversed 150 years of one-nation conservatism, and, as a result, the gap between rich and poor widened dramatically during the 'Thatcher years'. She was seen as the most divisive prime minister of the twentieth century, and although she was in power for only 11 years the divisions have yet to heal. She was determined to reduce public spending dramatically, especially on welfare and the National Health Service; she imposed government (some would say political) control over education; and she resolved to break the power of the trade unions, leading to a year-long miners' strike. Duffy's view of this era is perhaps best revealed in 'Fraud' and 'Weasel Words', a scathing attack on the ways in which politicians manipulate language.

Thatcher aroused strong reactions in different groups of people. She was seen as a hero by patriotic, anti-European nationalists, and by those who took advantage of the opportunity to become rich without the need for a social conscience (this is parodied in 'Making Money'). People with a concern for justice, or for the interests of women, minorities and the underprivileged, such as Carol Ann Duffy, typically loathed her. When Argentina invaded the Falkland Islands in 1982, she ordered British forces to retake the islands and won the title 'Iron Lady', of which she was proud.

Feminism

For centuries, women in European societies have enjoyed significantly fewer human rights than men. Responsibility for this lies principally with the medieval Christian Church, which decided to blame Eve, the **archetypal** woman, for the Fall of mankind. This scapegoating allowed men to seize control of the Church and political power in the Middle Ages. As a wife, a woman was the property of her husband. When societies began to move towards democracy in the nineteenth century, only men were given the vote. There were a number of respects in which women were discriminated against by the law, especially in regard to property rights, whereby only men were permitted to inherit. Women were not allowed to take university degrees in Britain until early in the twentieth century.

Women's suffrage

By the early nineteenth century this situation was beginning to be seen as unfair by some women, such as Mary Wollstonecraft, and the feminist movement slowly emerged. But it was not until the early twentieth century that the struggle for equal rights for women was forced onto the political agenda by the suffragette movement, which campaigned for women to be given the vote. The important role played by women in the First World War led to women over the age of 30 (and some younger ones) being given the vote in 1918, although it was 1928 before all women had the vote on an equal footing with men. (There are still parts of Switzerland that deny women the vote in some elections.)

Women's liberation

The women's movement received a new impetus in the 1960s and 1970s with the emergence of the feminist movement in the USA and elsewhere, and the writings of Germaine Greer (especially *The Female Eunuch*, published in 1970) and others began to have an impact. The magazine *Spare Rib* (the title is an ironic reference to the Bible story that Eve, the first woman, was created out of a spare rib from Adam, the first man) spread feminist ideas broadly, and irresistible political pressure began to be exerted by women, who, after all, represented more than half of the electorate. A series of legislative changes swept away some of the legal discrimination against women, but at the same time more radical feminists mounted a more fundamental challenge against the patriarchal structure and attitudes of society. Why, they argued, should a woman adopt her husband's surname on marriage? Why should she change her title from 'Miss' to 'Mrs' to denote ownership, when a man did not? Feminists adopted the title 'Ms' to apply to all women regardless of their marital status. Some even argued that men were unnecessary (a position adopted by a number of **personas** in Duffy's *The World's Wife*), arguing instead for lesbian households. Less radically, some questioned why women should be expected to present themselves as sex objects for men. Many women cut their hair short, symbolically burned their bras, stopped shaving their legs, refused to wear make-up and dressed the way they wanted to, which often meant in trousers.

Another line of attack was against prejudice embedded in linguistic usage: why should the head of a committee be a chair*man*? The campaign to promote gender-free language was ridiculed by some men as political correctness, but it drew attention to a hitherto-neglected form of discrimination. Although it is now customary to refer to all those in the acting profession as 'actors', for example, job descriptions such as 'actress', 'poetess' and 'lady-doctor' drew attention to the female gender of their holder. It is an irony that these 'marked forms' actually referred to the majority, as 51% of the population is female.

Reclaiming history

An important part of the feminist critique of society involved examining the roots of established prejudices. The Bible, classical **mythology** and fairy stories were all found to have deeply embedded anti-female prejudices, and some feminists worked to develop alternative mythologies. Lilith, the feisty first wife of Adam, was identified as an alternative to Eve; Angela Carter rewrote traditional fairy stories from a feminist perspective; Duffy herself has contributed to this process by revisiting a number of biblical and mythological stories in *The World's Wife*. Duffy refers in passing to the male domination of publishing (see 'Eurydice'), and in 1973 Virago Press was set up by a group of women with the aim of publishing women's writing; this was an important step towards equality of opportunity for women writers. Prior to this, many women had chosen to use their initials (A. S. Byatt and

U. A. Fanthorpe for example) to disguise the fact that they were female. In the nineteenth century, women authors such as Mary Ann Evans (writing as George Eliot) and Charlotte Brontë (writing as Currer Bell) had to adopt male names in order to be published. The writings of women began to complement the traditional works of 'DWEMs' (Dead White European Males) on examination syllabuses, although there is still some way to go before equality is achieved.

Sexism today

Although most of the legal discrimination against women has been removed, a significant number of contexts remain in which women are, in reality, far from equal. The continuing high level of violence against women committed by men, especially rape, indicates how much still needs to be done; for example, the continuing domination of the judiciary by men makes it difficult to secure convictions of rapists. Many women, especially in professions and business, find that there is still a 'glass ceiling' above which women cannot rise, and instances of discrimination and abuse in the workplace remain common.

The celebrated poet Sylvia Plath, who lived one generation before Duffy, found the pressure of balancing the roles of wife, mother and poet intolerable in the oppressive social milieu of the early 1960s, and consequently committed suicide. Duffy has succeeded in combining a slightly different set of roles, as partner, mother, poet and academic, and has in the process become one of the best-known, most distinctive and most respected poets in UK literary circles; yet she cannot, and does not, expect to receive any public accolades for exposing the hypocrisies and inadequacies of the UK establishment with its patriarchal attitudes, vested interests and 'old boy' networks.

Historical and mythological characters

Aesop	(c.620 BC–560 BC) Ancient Greek writer of **fables**
Armstrong, Sir Robert	(1927–) British Cabinet Secretary 1979–87 in Thatcher's government
Ashputtel	girl in a fairy tale; similar to Cinderella with the same rags to riches story
Barabbas	thief freed instead of Christ by Pontius Pilate
Brady, Ian	(1938–) partner in crime of Myra Hindley; together they killed children in the 1960s and buried them on Saddleworth Moor in Yorkshire; they are known as the 'Moors Murderers'
Brando, Marlon	(1924–2004) American film star; best known for his portrayal of a mafia boss in *The Godfather*
Braque, Georges	(1882–1963) prominent Cubist artist

Circe	witch in Homer's *The Odyssey*
Cleopatra	(69 BC–30 BC) last Queen of Egypt, seduced the Roman Mark Antony
Darwin, Charles	(1809–82) biologist who proposed the theory of evolution
Davis, Bette	(1908–89) American film star of the 1940s
Dean, James	(1931–55) American film star; a rebel idolised by teenage boys, he died aged only 24 in a car crash
Delilah	a woman from the Bible, she was married to Samson and deprived him of his strength by cutting his hair
Demeter	the ancient Greek goddess of fertility
Diana, Princess of Wales	(1961–97) the iconic 'people's princess' who died in a car crash in Paris
Ellis, Ruth	(1926–55) a murderer and the last woman to be hanged in Britain
Ernst, Max	(1891–1976) a prominent German **surrealist** painter, poet and founder member of the Dada movement
Eurydice	in Greek mythology she was the wife of Orpheus; when she died, Orpheus journeyed to the Underworld to rescue her, but failed in his attempt
Faust (Dr Faustus)	medieval German alchemist who sold his soul to the Devil in return for riches, power and forbidden knowledge; he was punished for overstepping the boundaries of man's knowledge
Freud, Sigmund	(1856–1939) Austrian psychoanalyst; many of his theories were based on sex
Garbo, Greta	(1905–90) iconic Hollywood actress of the 1920s and 1930s
Hathaway, Anne	(1556?–1623) Shakespeare's wife
Helen of Troy	in Greek mythology she was the wife of Menelaus; her abduction by Paris caused the Trojan War; hers was 'the face that launched a thousand ships' (Marlowe)
Henreid, Paul	(1908–92) American film star of the 1940s, star of *Now, Voyager*
Herod	(73 BC–4 BC) King of Judea at the time of Christ; ordered the slaughter of the infants in Bethlehem
Myra Hindley	(1942–2002) partner in crime of Ian Brady; together they are known as the 'Moors Murderers'
Icarus	in Greek mythology, Icarus was the son of Daedalus; they both escaped from captivity in Crete by flying, using wings held together with wax, but Icarus flew too close to the sun, the wax melted, and he fell into the sea and drowned
Jagger, Mick	(1943–) lead singer of the pop group the Rolling Stones
Juliet	tragic heroine of Shakespeare's *Romeo and Juliet*
Kinnock, Neil	(1942–) leader of the Labour Party 1983–92, during the Thatcher years

Kray Twins	Ronnie (1933–95) and Reggie (1933–2000), East End gangsters of the 1960s
Lazarus	man in the Bible brought back from the dead by Christ
Medusa	in Greek mythology she was one of the Gorgons, whose gaze could turn any living thing to stone
Midas	(seventh century BC) King of Phrygia (now part of Greece); celebrated for his 'golden touch' (everything he touched turned to gold) and for having ass's ears
Mona Lisa	'La Gioconda', the famous portrait painted by Leonardo da Vinci from 1503–06, depicts Lisa Gioconda, the wife of a Florentine merchant, known as 'Mona Lisa'. The painting is celebrated for Mona Lisa's enigmatic smile
Monroe, Marilyn	(1926–62) Hollywood film star and sex **symbol** of 1950s and 1960s
Nefertiti	(sixteenth century BC) Queen of Egypt
Oppenheim, Meret	(1913–85) female German-Swiss artist of the surrealist movement
Orpheus	in Greek mythology, a celebrated poet who played the lyre
Parkinson, Cecil	(1931–) Conservative politician who had an affair with Sara Keays, who bore his illegitimate child; a scandal of the 1980s
Penelope	in Greek mythology, the wife of Odysseus who awaits his return from the Trojan War for 20 years
Pontius Pilate	Roman governor of Judea at time of the death of Christ
Pope Joan	(allegedly pope 855–57) ninth-century pope who turned out to be a woman when she gave birth; she is probably mythical
Presley, Elvis	(1935–77) the 'king' of rock and roll
Pygmalion	Ancient Greek sculptor who created a statue so beautiful that he wished for it to come to life
Quasimodo	known as *The Hunchback of Notre Dame*, the English title of the novel *Notre-Dame de Paris* (1831) by Victor Hugo
Queen of Sheba	**legendary** queen, possibly from Ethiopia, who lived in biblical times
Radstone, Judith	(1925–2001) politically radical, left-wing bookseller
Rapunzel	girl in a fairy tale whose hair was so long and luxurious that when she threw it down from the tower where she was imprisoned, her prince was able to climb up it
Salome	biblical dancer who asked for, and was given, the head of John the Baptist on a platter
Sisyphus	Ancient Greek condemned to roll a boulder up a hill for eternity
Smith, Bessie	(1895–1937) celebrated American blues singer of the 1920s

Tantalus	in Greek mythology, he was punished by being offered food and drink which he could never quite reach
Thatcher, Margaret	(1925–) Conservative prime minister of the UK, 1979–90
Thetis	one of the Nereids in Greek mythology
Tiresias	character from Ancient Greek mythology who was turned into a woman for 7 years after he hit two copulating serpents with a stick; he was subsequently better known as a blind seer
Verlaine, Paul	(1844–96) French poet
Winkle, Rip van	character in a fairy tale by Washington Irving (1783–1859) who fell asleep for 20 years
Wray, Fay	(1907–2004) celebrated Hollywood actress of the 1930s and the victim in *King Kong*

Themes

The range of themes that appear in Duffy's poetry is wide, but there are a core group that recur regularly in a variety of forms.

Feminism/women

Contemporary life for girls and women is explored in many of Duffy's poems. The experiences she deals with range from rape and murder through bullying and marginalisation to contentment, often in a lesbian relationship. This theme becomes much more explicit and prominent in *The World's Wife*, which can be seen as a manifesto for late twentieth-century feminism.

Duffy generally presents girls as being more likely to be able to adapt, to be positive, to have ambitions and to make the best of the opportunities offered to them; boys are more likely to be inadequate, to fail to grow up, to hold unreflective prejudices or to resort to violence. Examples can be found in the following poems:

- murder — 'Psychopath'
- rape — 'Girl Talking'
- abuse — 'Lizzie, Six'; 'Stafford Afternoons'
- exploitation — 'Standing Female Nude'
- contentment — 'Girlfriends'
- girls vs. boys — 'Comprehensive'; 'Stealing'; 'Education for Leisure'; 'Descendants'

Alienation and nostalgia

Duffy writes 'All childhood is an emigration' in 'Originally', but not all emigrations are successful. Those who have suffered abuse or trauma are less likely to make the transition, but in general it seems that in Duffy's world men are more likely to remain fixated with their childhood through a reluctance to grow up or inadequacy. This is, however, not the only reason why young men are alienated from society: laziness, fecklessness and boredom all contribute (see particularly 'Stealing' and 'Education for Leisure').

Even when the transition to adulthood is successfully made, childhood memories retain their power. Nostalgia for schooldays seems to be especially important in Duffy's work. In a number of poems the transition from childhood to adulthood can be seen as a re-working of William Blake's concept of 'innocence and experience'. The change from the former to the latter can be sudden and terrifying, or it can happen gently and naturally. Examples can be found in the following poems:

- emigration from childhood — 'Liar'; 'Boy'; 'Model Village'; 'Psychopath'
- nostalgia in general — 'Nostalgia'; 'Liverpool Echo' ('As if nostalgia means you did not die'); 'Whoever She Was'
- nostalgia for schooldays — 'Head of English'; 'In Mrs Tilscher's Class'; 'The Good Teachers'; 'The Captain of the 1964 *Top of the Form* Team'
- change from innocence to experience — 'Stafford Afternoons' (sudden); 'Model Village' (subliminal); the persona in 'Litany' has moved on from the humiliation of that day, but it remains vivid in her mind

Public faces, private lives

Virtually all of Duffy's personas are characterised by the gap between their outward appearance and the inner reality, usually exposed through the interior **monologue**. This means that fear of discovery is another theme, because so many of Duffy's personas hide secrets, to various extents shocking. Their relationship to the public, judging world is therefore complex: they are often morally indifferent to it (in many cases, they seem entirely unaware of conventional morality), but they know that exposure will bring risk or worse. Examples can be found in 'Model Village', 'Fraud', 'Psychopath' and 'Liar'.

'The other country'

'The other country' is such an important concept for Duffy that she makes it the title of her third collection. It can literally be the other country from which an immigrant comes, or it can be the fantasy country to which the persona would like to escape. Everyone, Duffy seems to be saying, needs an alternative reality of some kind, either to escape to or to cling to in memory. Examples of a literal other country can be found in 'Foreign' and 'River'; examples of an imaginary other country can be found in 'In Your Mind', 'Dear Norman', 'Education for Leisure' and 'Big Sue and *Now, Voyager*'.

Relationships and love

A number of poems explore relationships from a wide range of viewpoints. Several, but not all, of these are about lesbian relationships, but Duffy is equally concerned with women who are cheated, betrayed or abused by men. Some of her love poems are **lyrical** and moving. Examples include 'Miles Away', 'Lovesick', 'Valentine', 'Adultery', 'Close', and 'Correspondents'.

Use and abuse of language

Duffy is clearly fascinated by language and often writes explicitly about it, including explicit references to grammatical points, e.g. verbs, nouns. She is especially concerned with the abuse of language, either for political ends, or to manipulate people's perceptions. For example:

- Political and misused language is dealt with in 'Weasel Words' and 'A Healthy Meal'.
- General examples are: 'That was/the wrong verb. This is only an abstract noun' ('Adultery'); 'A thin skin lies on the language' ('Moments of Grace'); 'Away and see the things that words give a name to, the flight/of syllables, wingspan stretching a noun' ('Away and See').
- 'Grammar of Light', a subtle and complex poem, compares the way grammar articulates the meaning of language with shades of light.

Numerous other examples can be found in '$', 'Poet for Our Times' and 'Making Money'.

Politics

Some poems are explicitly political or address controversial issues. Examples include:

- 'Selling Manhattan' — European colonialism
- 'Weasel Words' — lack of integrity of politicians
- 'Making Money' — Thatcherite obsession with greed
- 'The Dolphins' — animal rights
- 'A Healthy Meal' — vegetarianism
- 'Shooting Stars' — the Holocaust; racism
- 'Comprehensive' — racism

Religion

Duffy was brought up as a Roman Catholic and there are a number of references to Catholicism in her poems, such as Latin phrases and prayers. 'The Virgin Punishing the Infant' is an early example of a Duffy perspective on a Bible story and there are several more in *The World's Wife*, such as 'Delilah', 'Queen Herod' and 'Pilate's Wife'. 'Litany', 'Prayer' and 'Moments of Grace' all transfer religious ideas to a modern secular context. 'Elvis's Twin Sister' relocates the rock singer in a nunnery.

Reversal of expectation

It is characteristic of Duffy to set up situations in which the reader's expectations, based upon conventions and stereotypes, are demolished (this is a characteristic post-modernist device). Examples from the *Selected Poems* include 'The Dummy', in which the dummy has the dominant role in the relationship with the ventriloquist, and 'Model Village', in which the inhabitants of the village are not morally 'model'. *The World's Wife* contains many instances, generally by subverting a familiar story. Examples include 'Pope Joan', which is about a pope who does not believe a word of Christianity; 'Penelope', who is 'most certainly not waiting' for Odysseus; and 'The Kray Sisters', who are protecting women, not committing violent crimes.

Sex

Duffy is well known for her depictions of lesbian sex but her attitude towards sexuality is complex. Her poems include several examples of fulfilling heterosexual passion, lust and exploitative or abusive sex perpetrated by men upon women. Examples in *Selected Poems* include:

- 'Oppenheim's Cup and Saucer', 'Girlfriends' — lesbian sex
- 'Correspondents', 'Adultery' — heterosexual sex
- 'Close' — an interesting meditation upon sexual relationships — the gender of the two people involved is **ambiguous**, giving the poem universal application

In *The World's Wife* the references to sex are more explicit, e.g. 'Delilah', 'The Devil's Wife' and 'Mrs Quasimodo'.

Greek mythology

Greek mythology is an important source for Duffy in *The World's Wife*. This is partly because modern gender archetypes often derive from classical forebears. Alternatively, Duffy could be seen as attempting to set up an alternative set of myths.

Viewing Greek myths from a female perspective generally subverts their familiar **connotations**, e.g. 'Demeter' and 'Penelope'. 'Medusa' is treated differently because she is already a strong female, like 'Delilah' from the Bible story.

Language

Duffy's use of language is intelligent, original and challenging. Her tendency to use personas means that she has to adopt a wide variety of voices in her poetry, and she clearly enjoys the opportunities this offers her. She mimics styles, voices, accents and idioms with considerable skill, and to do so frequently employs **colloquialisms**, slang and even expletives. However, there is a style that appears to varying extents in a number of poems, and which can be seen as Duffy's own voice. It can be described as an elegant, matter-of-fact style that makes many of her poems easily

accessible, although often it includes subtleties that are not apparent on a first reading. This style is most easily identified in the poems that have a third-person narrator who can conventionally be assumed to be 'the poet', e.g. 'Nostalgia' and 'The Grammar of Light'. However, it is worth noting that there is no reason why what might be seen as Duffy's own voice is any less constructed than the other voices she adopts, and just another persona.

Duffy has been accused of using 'unpoetic' language, but in fact she is capable of writing with a lyrical tenderness, for example: 'I have learned/the solemn laws of joy and sorrow, in the distance/between morning's frost and firefly's flash at night' ('Selling Manhattan'); 'I hold you closer, miles away,/inventing love, until the calls of the nightjars/interrupt and turn what was to come, was certain,/into memory' ('Miles Away').

Monologues

The vast majority of Duffy's poems are in the form of a monologue. Even in the cases where another voice is heard, it is rarely more than an interjection, and it is often unclear whether the monologue is being voiced aloud or whether it is internal. Many are delivered in 'real-time', as if the persona were commenting on events as they occur, in the form of a non-grammatical, stream-of-consciousness sequence of images, events and thoughts. Examples of this can be found in 'Psychopath' and 'The Captain of the 1964 *Top of the Form* Team'.

Other monologues seem to have been prepared beforehand by the persona and flow smoothly and grammatically, e.g. 'Weasel Words', 'Selling Manhattan' and 'Dear Norman'. Some monologues, such as 'Litany' and 'Stafford Afternoons' from *Selected Poems*, are retrospective accounts which look back on events with a degree of detachment. In *The World's Wife* this becomes the established style.

Duffy often surprises and shocks the reader by making abrupt transitions between one style and another. These changes generally reflect the developing subject matter of the poem. The stream-of-consciousness monologues, in particular, frequently switch from full sentences to staccato phrases or words. Examples of poems which include such transitions are 'Psychopath' and 'Comprehensive'. In *The World's Wife*, shock is achieved by the unexpected appearance of 'fuck' in 'Delilah' and 'Mrs Quasimodo'.

Stanza transitions

Most of Duffy's poems are divided, apparently conventionally, into **stanzas** that are often regular in length. The stanzas are often **end-stopped**, but not always. Duffy uses stanza-transitions to achieve a variety of effects, e.g. in 'Stafford Afternoons', where this device regulates the pace at which the reader reads, and the last two stanzas run swiftly on, mimicking the child's panic; see also 'Adultery' and, in *The World's Wife*, 'Mrs Lazarus' and 'Little Red-Cap'.

Another device which Duffy employs is to place a word ambiguously at the end of a line so that its meaning is divided between the line it completes and the line it starts. This is exaggerated when it is used at a stanza break. For example, in 'Standing Female Nude', 'It makes me laugh. His name' is clear enough, until reading the first line of the next stanza, which changes this to 'His name/is Georges'. Similarly, in 'River' the first stanza ends 'there, nailed to a tree, is proof. A sign', which seems complete, but the beginning of the next stanza makes this become 'A sign/in new language brash on a tree'.

Personas

A number of Duffy's characters can be described as inadequate in one way or another: they have not grown up; cannot cope with reality or relationships; break the law or delude themselves. Giving voices to these people is a central part of Duffy's poetry, but it is also the cause of a tantalising feature of the poems. These characters could never discuss their inner life with any other, so how can they conduct such lucid, self-knowing monologues? Is Duffy cheating or interfering, not only with their language register, but also with the subtlety of their self-knowledge? In many cases it is impossible to disentangle the voice of persona from its manipulation by Duffy, and often a change of language will give a clue that the perspective or voice has subtly changed. The fairground worker in 'Psychopath' is a good example; his usually impoverished utterances give way to a poetic and perceptive observation: 'These streets are quiet, as if the town has held its breath/to watch the Wheel go round above their dreary homes.' In 'Model Village' the persona's voice suddenly changes at the end: 'Did you/see the frog? Frogs say *Croak*...The Vicar is nervous/of parrots, isn't he? Miss Maiden is nervous/of Vicar and the Farmer is nervous of everything.'

Surprises

Duffy plays games with our expectations and enjoys catching us out. She is constantly trying to make the reader see things afresh and reconsider old connections. Some examples of such surprising images and **juxtapositions** are: 'showing you how the trees/in the square think in birds, telepathise.' ('The Grammar of Light'); 'I pause/in this garden, breathing the colour thought is/before language into still air' ('Miles Away').

Images and motifs

Mirrors

Examples can be found in 'Recognition' and 'Psychopath'. Mirrors play an important role in Duffy's poetry: characters often look at themselves in mirrors, as

a form of self-validation or as a window into their souls. In 'Mrs Beast', there is the observation that 'The moon was a hand-mirror breathed on by a Queen'.

Catalogues

Catalogues are like litanies and invoke an element of ritual; the monotony of their intonation is a reminder of church services. Examples include 'Litany', 'The Captain of the 1964 *Top of the Form* Team' and 'Making Money'; in *The World's Wife* there are 'Circe' and 'Frau Freud'.

Film

Examples include 'Psychopath', 'Big Sue and *Now, Voyager*' and 'Miles Away'. Duffy perhaps employs these because film was, arguably, the dominant cultural medium of the period about which she writes, and particularly influenced her personas.

Paintings

Examples include 'Standing Female Nude' and 'Oppenheim's Cup and Saucer'.

Music

Examples include '$' and 'The Captain of the 1964 *Top of the Form* Team'. Pop music is another of the formative cultural influences upon personas from the 1960s onwards; for many people, pop songs are indelibly associated with important experiences in their lives, as for 'The Captain'.

Notes on the poems
Selected Poems
From *Standing Female Nude* (1985)

'Girl Talking'

A moving, elliptical account of the rape and death of a young Moslem girl set in an ethnic community. The title could stand for many of Duffy's poems.

'Comprehensive'

This is an important early poem because of its explicit attention to racism, alienation, gender and education — all key themes in Duffy's work. British education was re-organised in the 1960s. Comprehensive schools were introduced, in which children from all backgrounds were educated together. However, Duffy's choice of title is ambiguous, because she is referring both to the school and to the concept of comprehensiveness — inclusiveness — or its absence, as well as to the wide range of ethnic backgrounds and political and personal attitudes of the children in the poem. The poem gives a picture of how many British schools (and towns) have become multiracial, of the tensions involved, and of the radically different attitudes of various groups.

All the reader is given is the voices of seven children, and we have to infer the circumstances in which these mini-monologues arise. It is probably easiest to picture the poem as a series of interviews; two of the characters start by stating their name. It is certainly, in some sense, a series of snapshots of students. Alternatively, they could be brief autobiographies written as a class exercise.

This poem is typical of Duffy in several ways: the personas speak for themselves, and Duffy expects the reader to employ knowledge and sensitivity to work out what is going on. The children condemn themselves, or otherwise, by their thoughts and the language they use to express them. We have to deduce what we can about the children's gender and ethnic background.

Persona/stanza 1

The persona is an African girl, possibly from Ghana, where Kwani-kwani is played. She is homesick, nostalgic, but slightly positive nevertheless. She sounds young and in some ways naive; although she misses her home in Africa, she has learned to cope, with the help of her mother, by remembering what they have left behind. The **tone** is one of acceptance and a degree of calm.

Persona/stanza 2

Wayne is a 14-year-old British boy. He is virtually monosyllabic and supports the National Front, a political party principally composed of mindless racists such as him. His intellectual horizons are watching videos and football matches, and he has no ambition whatsoever. Wayne is too stupid and lazy to use sentences. His politics are as repugnant as his view of girls: he bashes 'pakis' and pulls down girls' knickers. His utterances are ungrammatical and employ the impoverished vocabulary of thugs. No process of thought impedes the **clichéd** prejudices that he utters.

Persona/stanza 3

The persona is a Pakistani teenager of uncertain gender. She/he is nostalgic about the home she/he has left behind, but her/his attitude to the new life in Britain is not clear.

Persona/stanza 4

Michelle is an unambitious British girl, semi-illiterate, inarticulate and racist. Michelle thinks her name is boring, or possibly her life, or both. She has not lost her virginity yet, but her ambitions do not extend beyond working in Safeways and marriage, although not to anyone 'dark'.

Persona/stanza 5

Ejaz is a Westernised, Urdu-speaking Moslem boy; he is attacked by another 'Moslem boy' because he does not have such a fundamentalist view about eating pork, or because he naively imagined 'They' would not serve pork to Moslems, but the two boys become friends through finding what they have in common in the face of the 'They' of the first line.

Persona/stanza 6

The persona is another racist British boy. 'My sister went out with one' (i.e. someone from an ethnic minority) is a racist dismissal. His racism is subtler than Wayne's — 'I'd like to be mates', he claims, although we may not believe him. He does at least want a job, even if it is in the army. The phrase 'no choice' suggests that he might have liked to have had alternatives, but he cannot imagine any.

Persona/stanza 7

An ambitious Pakistani teenager is the persona of this stanza; the tale of the milk suggests that she/he is timid, and did not dare ask for clarification. Despite this, the persona is ambitious and optimistic, the note on which the poem arguably ends.

The girls tend to be more ambitious than the boys, but, more dramatically, the British children are all in varying degrees racist, unreflective and lacking in ambition, indicated by their impoverished vocabulary and ideas. The only evidence for identifying and assessing the personas comes from their own speech. The immigrants all speak more grammatically, are more reflective and sensitive and employ a more sophisticated vocabulary. They have all overcome hardship of some kind, but all seem to have been strengthened by it (and none actually seems to have been the victim of any vicious attack). They are also aware of the educational opportunity they have been offered, and seek to make the best of it. The British students, by contrast, make no reference to school, education or qualifications; if they intend to have jobs at all, they aren't jobs that are dependent on academic achievement. The simplicity of their language and grammar reflects their refusal to accept any education or to think about the prejudices within which they have been brought up.

Themes

The central themes of the poem — racism, alienation, gender and education — are all key themes of Duffy's work. Other themes include the importance of seizing opportunities and of having goals; deracination; translocation; and the difficulties facing immigrants in a hostile culture.

References and allusions

- 'Tutumantu', 'Kwani-kwani', line 1: African games
- 'the National Front', line 9: a racist British political party that wants all immigrants to be sent back to their countries of origin
- 'Masjid', line 14: Moslem temple

'Head of English'

Partly a semi-nostalgic account of remembered schooldays, but also a biting **parody** of a head of English of the old school, uptight and not really in sympathy with the poet she has invited in for 'an outside view'. The poem can be seen as a parody of old-fashioned views on what poetry is and the process of writing it, as is suggested by comments such as 'verse hot from the press', and references to Kipling and Keats, who are usually regarded as 'traditional' poets.

'Lizzie, Six'

A disturbing **dialogue** between an adult man and a young girl whom he is intent on abusing.

'Education for Leisure'

Duffy is interested in education and regularly writes about school experiences. This poem extends the idea by considering the use that the persona has made of his/her education. Mass education has been one of the great achievements of the nineteenth and twentieth centuries. After 1944, all children in the UK were entitled to a free education that would teach them to make constructive use of the leisure time that an increasingly affluent society would offer. In the poem, the idea of 'Education for Leisure' is deeply ironic; the persona does not have a job, is living on the 'dole', and as a consequence is permanently bored.

However, it could be argued that Duffy is being critical of the 'dole trap' and questioning whether education has prepared the persona for anything. Perhaps his/her psychopathic tendencies are a product of failures in the system.

The persona

As is typical of a Duffy poem, there is no external evidence of the gender of the persona, and the reader must start by forming a judgement. In this case, the presence of violence, self-glorifying fantasies and lack of ambition might suggest that the persona is male; the references to Gloucester, a male character in *King Lear*, and God, who is usually described as male, support this. The persona certainly matches Duffy's typical representation of inadequate young males: his/her education has prepared him/her only for the dole; he/she has no real self-knowledge, and a flippant attitude to the violent acts that he/she imagines and describes. Nevertheless, as is often the case, Duffy gives no categorical indication of the persona's gender, and the reader is left to judge.

The persona is cool, relaxed and almost flippant to the extent that the reader initially wonders whether he/she is merely joking out of boredom, although as the poem progresses it becomes clear that this is not the case. Dissociation is apparent: his/her tone does not relate to his/her actions. This is behaviour typical of psychopaths, who are of great interest to Duffy (see 'Psychopath'). It is unsettling

to have such a subject described in this casual way, and it establishes a distance between the persona and what we would consider 'normal' behaviour.

What nags at the reader is the language **register** employed by the persona; he/she shows occasional evidence of being educated and fluent, which raises the question not addressed at all in the poem: is he/she unemployed through force of circumstance, or from choice? Does the existence of the dole make it too easy not to bother to get a job? There are flashes of cleverness: 'We did that at school. Shakespeare. It was in/another language and now the fly is in another language.' In *King Lear* (IV.1.38–39), Gloucester says: 'As flies to wanton boys are we to the gods,/They kill us for their sport.' The persona not only attended school, but took enough interest to recall this sentiment from Shakespeare. He/she is no fool. Shakespeare is not really written 'in/another language', although many school-children think it is; the fly has now been metaphorically translated into the language of death. This reference is connected to the persona playing God, and suggests death, fatalism and hopelessness. Flies are also associated with disease and decay.

Similarly, 'I see that it is good' is an echo of the Bible. In Genesis, God peri-odically pauses to reflect upon his work, e.g. 'and God saw that it was good' (1:10). In line 3, the persona informs the reader that he/she would 'play God', and he/she compares the act of murdering the goldfish with an act of God: it is a similar arbitrary power over the fate of another. The cat, a more wily adversary, can slip away; the budgerigar in its cage cannot, and is therefore supposedly 'panicking'. It is, of course, fantasy to suppose that a bird could react in such a way, but psychopaths derive much of their satisfaction from the fear they inspire in potential victims.

These glimpses of the persona's character give an impression of immaturity and inadequacy, as well as a feeling that he/she is not appreciated, although possibly at school he/she was told that he/she was talented or had ability. He/she may have tried jobs and been disappointed that his/her qualities were not recognised (cf. 'The Captain of the 1964 *Top of the Form* Team'). Quotations supporting these concerns include:

- 'I have had enough of being ignored and today/I am going to play God' — a revealing comment about the persona's psychological state.
- 'I am a genius. I could be anything at all' (cf. 'Psychopath': 'I could be anything with my looks') — this is presumably wishful thinking.
- 'But today I am going to change the world./Something's world' — there is some self-knowledge here: he/she cannot really change the world, merely interfere with that of a creature or a person.
- 'They don't appreciate my autograph' — he/she is required to sign to receive his/her dole money, and it is pure fantasy to imagine that this administrative signature in any way resembles the 'autograph' of a celebrity.

- 'I dial the radio/and tell the man he's talking to a superstar' — radio phone-ins are a way for unimportant people to gain a moment's celebrity, but the host of this show is not taken in; the persona seems surprisingly calm about this rejection.

The ending

The last line of the poem introduces an unusual twist. The sudden, direct address to the reader is a terrible shock and completely changes the reader's response. The internal monologue, which has so far been the crazed fantasy of the bored young persona, suddenly becomes horribly real: this psychopath is holding a bread-knife and is touching the arm of a human being. There is a direct threat to the reader, the 'you'. We are reminded of the poem's opening: 'Today I am going to kill something.' It is a huge step from a goldfish to a human being, but we are uncertain enough of the persona, because of the dissociated tone of the poem, to be unable to judge whether murder is a real possibility or not.

Style and form

The poem is written in the form of an internal monologue, delivered in 'real time' in the present tense but with no apparent audience until the sudden introduction of 'your' in the final line. It may be part of the persona's fantasy to imagine he/she is important enough for people to be interested in his/her thoughts — the references to 'genius', 'superstar' and 'autograph' suggests that the persona has a high opinion of him/herself but is ignored by society. The language is generally grammatical, but in simple sentences and featuring isolated words ('Anything', 'Shakespeare') and with unambitious vocabulary. Each of the stanzas is end-stopped and deals with a different set of ideas.

Themes

The poem is about the emptiness of the persona's life and his/her failure to respond morally to his/her situation or his/her actions. Duffy asks us to consider whether his/her education is at fault (unusually, we learn nothing else of the persona's background or past). Would the persona, or the world, have been better off in an earlier age when he/she would have worked in the fields all day and would have remained illiterate? The themes also include: the irony of the ineffectiveness of education, given the high hopes that were invested in the potential of education to widen the horizons of working-class children; the inadequacy of young men, and their tendency to retreat into fantasy and violence; the horror of boredom (see also 'Stealing'); loneliness; isolation.

References and allusions

- 'talent', line 8: breath condensed on the cold glass enables the persona to write his/her name and view his/her breath as a 'talented' emanation of his/her spirit
- 'the bog', line 13: the toilet
- 'the budgie', line 14: a budgerigar, a domesticated bird kept in a cage

- 'the two miles into town/for signing on', lines 15–16: i.e. signing onto the dole (unemployment benefit); the persona is unemployed and living on state benefits

'I Remember Me'

This is a reflection upon sadness and isolation. Note the unhappy, empty **diction**: 'despair', 'wordless'. The poem ends with a haunting and depressing observation on love.

'Whoever She Was'

The poem is about the nostalgia of an old woman looking back over her life. An old flickering film, of the type used for historical documentaries, appears to represent her life. The end of the poem suggests that the persona is either actually or metaphorically dead.

'Dear Norman'

- Themes: fantasy; escape; appearance and reality; the other country; control
- Motifs: window-pane
- Persona: unclear — perhaps middle-aged man?
- Context: present-day Britain
- Form: reflective internal monologue; four regular 5-line stanzas plus 1-line *envoi*
- Style: fluent, grammatical, quite formal register

The title is interestingly ambiguous. It could be a description of the persona ('Dear Norman, he's such a sweetie') or the salutation of a letter the persona is writing. The poem is about fantasy and escape from humdrum, everyday existence; it is also about the exercise of power over another, although in this case the power is not threatening (compare with 'In Your Mind'). The quotation is the first line of a poem by Pablo Neruda (hence naming the boy 'Pablo'), which, surprisingly, is about the body of a woman ('*cuerpo de mujer*' means 'body of a woman'). The concluding 'Tomorrow I shall deal with the dustman' reminds us of the power fantasies of 'Psychopath' and 'Education for Leisure'. The poem is written in a fluent — in places convoluted — style, and there are erotic overtones in the sensuous description of the boy's body.

'Talent'

This short poem is about language and its relationship with thought. Unusually, Duffy addresses the audience directly.

'$'

This is an ironic reference to pop music: the meaningless lyrics quoted in the poem are converted into dollars for their performers. It is perhaps a comment on how language can be emptied of meaning (see 'Weasel Words').

'Liverpool Echo'

- Themes: nostalgia; loss
- Persona: none
- Context: Liverpool, present day, looking back
- Form: third-person observation/reflection by the poet; two end-stopped 4-line stanzas, followed by two 3-line stanzas that run on

The title is that of a Liverpool newspaper. This poem is nostalgic for the Liverpool of 1962. Mathew Street is the location of the Cavern, the club where The Beatles began their careers in 1962. The Beatles did a version of *Ain't She Sweet*. Duffy seems to be suggesting that the city, like so many of her characters, cannot move on from its moment of fame (compare especially 'The Captain of the 1964 *Top of the Form* Team'). The ending brings us abruptly to a present which does not hold the excitement and potential of 1962: 'And wait.'

'Standing Female Nude'

- Themes: feminism; point of view
- Motifs: art
- Persona: woman, artist's model and prostitute
- Context: Paris, 1908
- Form: internal monologue; four regular 7-line stanzas
- Style: stream of ideas, some phrases grammatical, many ungrammatical

The French cubist painter Georges Braque (1882–1963) painted a picture entitled *Standing Female Nude*; this poem is an imaginative recreation of the circumstances of its painting seen through the eyes of the persona, the artist's nude model. There are numerous suggestions that make it clear she is a prostitute. Duffy draws parallels between the model's sitting for the artist and prostitution, such as the phallic image of him dipping his brush, and her reaction when he's finished: 'I say/Twelve francs and get my shawl.' She is distanced from what she has done, and comments that 'He possesses me on canvas'. The artist is attracted to the model ('stiffens for my warmth'), but the arrangement is purely mercenary for her. Her dismissive final comment reminds us that cubist art was not universally appreciated, and made no attempt at the accurate depiction of its subjects. Note a typical Duffy ambiguity at the end of the second stanza: 'It makes me laugh. His name', which in full is 'His name/is Georges.' The effect is emphasised by the stanza break. The ambiguity emphasises the fact that she is not in awe of this famous artist.

'Oppenheim's Cup and Saucer'

This poem continues Duffy's use of works of art from the early twentieth century as her inspiration (see also 'The Virgin Punishing the Infant'). Meret Oppenheim was a German–Swiss Surrealist (1913–85); the fur-lined cup (named 'Le Déjeuner

en Fourrure', 1936) was her most famous work. This is an explicitly erotic lesbian poem: the cup and saucer image suggests two parts fitting together, and they have round, female shapes.

'Shooting Stars'

A moving poem about the Holocaust. The names listed are Jewish. Note the juxtaposition of David, the last of the list, with the stars (of David) which all the prisoners wore. '[R]agged gape of fear' is an echo of 'rape', and is recalled by 'gap' in the next line. Duffy is particularly interested in the contrast between the desperate victims, the nonchalance of the young soldiers, and the indifference of later generations, indicated by the children who 'run to their toys' after the lesson on the Holocaust. 'Remember' is an echo of *Hamlet*.

'The Dolphins'

This sad poem is about a pair of dolphins held in captivity by 'a man' who represents all those who imprison others or treat them cruelly; the dolphins represent all those who are not free. There are clear echoes of 'Selling Manhattan': the dolphin has a similar intuitive understanding of its element, and knows that its world has been destroyed by humans. The dolphin clings to the love of its partner, but 'There is no hope'. In place of the authenticity of their ocean and their lives 'There is a plastic toy'. Duffy concludes: 'There is a man and our mind knows we will die here.'

'A Healthy Meal'

A group of wealthy diners eat in a pretentious and expensive restaurant. The title is of course ironic: these gourmet meals are likely to make the eaters obese, and the slaughter involved in their preparation can be seen as morally unhealthy. This is an unusually direct and bitter attack upon a group of people, and pulls no punches. Equally unusually, there is no persona to mediate the assault: the words come directly from the poet and we can reasonably assume that these are Duffy's own views.

'The gourmet' is the opening phrase of the poem, making quite clear who Duffy's target is. Gourmets can be defined as connoisseurs of good food with discriminating palates. But they are often viewed as rich (because gourmet food is prohibitively expensive), greedy, self-indulgent and pretentious. The poem is certainly contemptuous and hostile towards them.

The poem is also about language: in particular, the elaborate **euphemisms** which gourmets employ to disguise the reality of what is being eaten, which constitutes a private language. In this sense it is a poem about abuse of language, and words not meaning what they seem: compare with 'Weasel Words'.

Much of the poem is in the form of elaborate metaphors. For example, cow brains are a delicacy for a gourmet. The metaphor 'tastes the secret dreams of cows' suggests that, by eating brains 'tossed lightly in garlic' (a pretentious way of saying 'cooked'), the gourmet might imagine that he/she is able to share the cow's dreams. This is mischief on Duffy's part, because gourmets are famously indifferent to the creatures they eat. Alternatively, Duffy is revealing the functions of the organ, which gourmets ignore or sanitise. The metaphor shows the poet's sympathy for the cows, in contrast to the indifference of the gourmets, and is similar to the hearts and tongues references later in the poem.

This sanitisation can be seen in the instruction to 'Alter calf to veal in four attempts' (line 13). This is an example of a well-known word game in which players change one letter at a time, to make a new word at each stage, and transform 'calf' to 'veal'. The solution is:

- CALF — young cow
- CALL — it is called to the slaughterhouse
- CELL — it is kept like a prisoner in a cell
- VELL — the stomach of a calf, used for making rennet
- VEAL — the sanitised name given to slaughtered calf

This is a word game, but for the calf it is deadly enough. The new name disguises the reality of the blood and butchery: 'brutally butchered young cow' would be a less appealing, but more honest, description on a menu. When Duffy says 'This is the power of words', she is continuing the same point, with more examples, of which 'lights' (lungs) is the most striking. Vegetarians often campaign to have accurate descriptions placed on restaurant menus in place of pretentious, misleading (often French) words.

Lines 1–2, 'These hearts knew/no love and on their beds of saffron rice they lie/beyond reproach' is an example of **anthropomorphism**. The human heart is identified with love and romance, and although the same can hardly be said of sheep hearts, Duffy wants to stress the 'humanity' of the slaughtered animals as much as she can. Unlike the humans who eat them, she seems to be saying, these creatures cannot be reproached for any moral failings. It is possible that the animals knew no love because they were treated badly. Note the repeated attempts to place the animals in human contexts: 'they lie' (line 7) and they are on 'pure white cloth' (line 12), ironic comparisons with how human corpses are laid out.

The last line is particularly stark: 'Death moves in the bowels' is reminiscent of 'Meat is murder', a well-known vegetarian slogan. Duffy wants to remind the reader (even if there is no point in reminding the gourmets) of the truth of what they are eating. 'You are what you eat' is a vicious, bitter summary of her view, and puts a shocking new spin on this cliché, which usually refers to dieting or healthy meals. The utterances are short and stark, the words short and hard.

Style and form

The poem is a series of observations of the diners rather than a narrative. Because it is not in the form of a monologue, it reads more like a conventional poem. The

narrator employs elaborate metaphors to describe the situation being observed. There is no narrative structure, so the interest is maintained by depicting the diners unattractively ('The woman chewing suckling pig', 'A fat man') and revealing the horror of the meals by, interestingly, generally avoiding the use of blunt language. The living nature of the now-dead animals is alluded to subtly: 'the language of tongues', 'swish of oxtails', 'secret dreams', 'something which once flew'. There are several such references to sounds, both of animals and diners: 'Capped teeth chatter', 'leg saddle and breast bleat', 'gag the groans'. The language is in an elevated register and is grammatical, with a couple of exceptions, which derive impact from this deviation, e.g. 'Blood', 'Belch'. The poem is written in 4-line stanzas, most of which are end-stopped, a form often employed by Duffy. Arguably, it has the effect of meeting the reader's expectations of a conventional poem — expectations that are subverted by the absence of any regular rhyme or metre.

Themes

The themes are: vegetarianism; the hypocrisy of the euphemistic language used to describe meat (see 'Weasel Words'); the implied deadening effect that the consumption of meat must have on the sensitivities of the eater.

There is no direct evidence of Catholicism in the poem, but the Roman Catholic Church has traditionally been indifferent to the suffering of animals (see Genesis and Thomas Aquinas). It is, however, possible to read the whole poem in a Catholic light: the gourmets stand accused (ironically, in view of the church's attitude to animals) of the culpable slaughter of innocent animals (note the recurring image of the sacrificial lamb in Christianity); 'absolve guilt', 'Blood' and 'wipe the evidence' could be described as Catholic images. The white cloth is a reminder of the Communion cloth, and the comparison of blood with wine reminds the reader of the Catholic mass. It is also possible to see a comparison between the seriousness and rituals of the gourmets and those of a religious service.

The poem is also a social comment on people who ostentatiously choose to spend large amounts of money on food when millions are starving; a comment on the gourmet's indifference to the suffering of animals; the abuse of language, which is manipulated to disguise the reality of what is being eaten, and how words don't mean what they seem, and have had their meaning sucked out (compare to 'Weasel Words').

References and allusions

- 'pinkies', line 4: little finger; a diner showed his/her class by holding out the little finger while eating or drinking
- 'fingerbowls', line 4: small bowls in which delicate diners rinsed their fingers after touching food
- 'claret', line 8: a fine red wine made in the Bordeaux region

- 'armagnac', line 10: a type of brandy, often used for cooking
- 'tripe', line 14: cooked stomach lining of an ox or cow
- 'lights', line 14: lungs of sheep, bullocks or pigs
- 'offal', line 19: edible internal parts of an animal, such as heart, liver and tongue

'And Then What'

A deceptively simple poem that summarises human life: work, fatigue, a brief moment of love and compassion, and then death. And then what?

From *Selling Manhattan* (1987)

'Dies Natalis'

This is one of Duffy's longest poems. The themes are continuity over time, re-incarnation and the essence of a being. The Latin title means 'the day of birth'. In the first section, set in the time of Cleopatra in ancient Egypt, the persona is a black cat (when the cat was revered as sacred). In the next, she is a seabird, possibly an albatross, and we are reminded of Coleridge's *The Rime of the Ancient Mariner*. In the third section, set approximately in the present day, the persona is male, and retells in glimpses the story of how his love blossomed and then waned, ending in his lover's death (probably from cancer). Finally, the persona is reborn as a new baby and, echoing Wordsworth, predicts that he/she will lose his/her memories of the archetypal, heroic passage through time which he/she has already experienced.

'The Dummy'

This poem is based on another reversal of expectation and giving voice to the dumb. The ventriloquist's dummy (which usually exists only to pass on its owner's words) develops a voice of its own, and is scathing about the inadequacies of the human.

'Model Village'

The title is, of course, ambiguous. At one level, it refers to those tourist attractions, scattered across Britain, where an entire village is reproduced in miniature for the amusement of children. More relevant, of course, is the suggestion that this is a 'model' village in the sense of normality and expected behaviour, and this is the expectation that Duffy delights in overturning.

The narrator could be a child visiting the physical model village. Alternatively, the instructions in the poem ('See the cows', 'Notice the horse') and phrases such as 'Hens say Cluck' sound like a children's book, and both these and the question tags ('don't they', 'isn't he') could suggest an adult talking to a child. She/he observes the unreality of the scene that has been constructed and imagines what might be going on inside the minds of the model people. (Is the poem really the imaginings of a child? Or is Duffy mischievously suggesting what the thoughts might be of the

real people who might live in such a village? Or is she anthropomorphising the models?)

The poem is about the contrast between the narrator's naive and **stereotypical** image of the inhabitants of the village, and the troubling reality of their secret lives (secret because, through guilt, they do not share them, and because, as inanimate models, they are incapable of sharing them — this ambiguity runs through the poem). It is a latter-day version of William Blake's idea of 'innocence and experience'.

The narrator

The innocence and naivety of the narrator are immediately apparent. Note how the poem starts with an imperative, as if he/she is addressing an audience (an accompanying adult, perhaps), although the poem reads like another internal monologue. The narrator repeats, with a childlike matter-of-factness, the stereotypical elements of the scene. But whereas he/she can be confident that, for example, the cat says '*Miaow*', humans are much less predictable. The simple statements, the childlike language and the naive questions all suggest the voice of a child or of an adult addressing a very young child.

In lines 55–57 the main narrator abruptly changes character. 'The Grocer has a parrot…/…The Vicar is nervous/of parrots, isn't he?' begins as another naive comment, but how could the narrator possibly know that the Vicar is nervous of the parrot, no doubt because it might repeat what he says aloud when he is indulging in his erotic fantasies? There is no way that the child could think this: it is a classic Duffian conceit, in which the persona of the narrator suddenly merges with that of the knowing poet, given away by the 'isn't he?' at the end of the line. This prepares us for the introduction of the final persona, who is arguably Duffy herself, the wise Librarian who hears and chronicles the foibles of all those around her.

Miss Maiden

Miss Maiden murdered her mother. Her name suggests that she is still a virgin (a maiden is still in possession of an intact maidenhead, or hymen) and reminds us of the phrase 'old maid', i.e. a woman who never married, and is presumed to be frustrated, crotchety or out of touch as a consequence. She had a suitor once, but her mother disapproved, and presumably prevented them from marrying (how?): '*she had more patience*'. Finally he gave up and went away. In the saddest line of the poem, Miss Maiden then looked at herself in the mirror (always an important source of validation in Duffy) and '*saw her grey hair, her lips of reproach*', i.e. saw that she was turning into her mother. Her mother cruelly exulted in the lover's departure, and Miss Maiden dismissively responds, having heard it so many times before, '*Yes, Mother, yes. Drink it all up.*' Ironically, she has finally learned her lesson this time, but not in the way her mother thinks. With whom do your sympathies lie?

The story is told economically, ungrammatically and in a matter-of-fact manner: it was a long time in the past, and Miss Maiden is resigned now to living the remainder of her life alone, but is still satisfied that she finally took action. The style contrasts with the other confessions, which are more grammatical and fluent.

The Farmer

The Farmer has had a disquieting vision, of which he seems in some obscure way to be ashamed. His confession is enigmatic, and it is hard to be certain, but he probably experienced a religious revelation of some sort. '*I'm searching for something*' is ambiguous; he could possibly be looking simply for an explanation, or for some meaning in his life. The vision frightened him just as it did the animals; why is he unable to talk about it? Does he see it as in some way personal, a reflection on his own failings?

The Vicar

The Vicar has a sadomasochistic fantasy that he is a naughty choirboy and that he will be spanked by an imaginary choirmistress. This particular sexual disorder — the desire to be beaten for sexual satisfaction — is allegedly so common in England that the French call it 'the English vice'. The Vicar's fantasy is a more extreme form, because he also desires to regress to boyhood, and has therefore shaved his legs (and, presumably, his pubic hair, because when he has an erection that too is described as '*Smooth, pink naughtiness*'). There probably is no choirmistress, and may never have been, so his entire sexual life is probably sublimated into this fantasy. Church of England vicars are not required to be celibate (unlike Roman Catholic clergy), but many are unmarried and the stereotype of a sexually inadequate or perverted vicar is a common one. He is nervous of the parrot, of course, because he fears that, if it hears him vocalise his fantasies, it will repeat them before an audience.

Lines 35–36, 'There's the church....', refers to a children's game in which the intertwined fingers of two hands represent a church and a steeple; inverted, the finger-ends represent people inside.

The Librarian

He/she is the repository of the secrets of the villagers, which is his/her secret. As in so many other cases, there is no external evidence of the persona's gender, and the internal evidence is of tone and nuance only. Village librarians, though, are stereo-typically female. The role of a silent listener who stores everyone's secrets is also, arguably, more often associated with women. This persona differs from the previous ones because of her assurance; she has no guilty secret, and perhaps merely enjoys the power derived from knowing and keeping the secrets of others; 'like a doctor on his rounds' suggests both authority and confidential knowledge. However, it may also be the case that she is not really interested in real lives, and prefers the orderliness of fiction. Some have identified Duffy with this character, in view of her ability to peek inside the lives of the silent and expose their secrets. The final line, '*the books in everyone's head are stranger...*', could be a subheading for Duffy's poetry.

Style and form

The form is regular: the main persona narrates in 8-line stanzas, and each of the other characters speaks in 9-line stanzas. As is customary in Duffy's poetry, italics indicate any voice other than the persona's. There is a good deal of **enjambement**, and it is occasionally ambiguous, as in the Farmer's monologue: 'Even the animals stiffened in fright. Look' — this is grammatically linked to the next line, and is **rhetorical**, but clings to the description of the animals, as if the reader were being directed to observe them. Each persona has his/her own distinctive style. The main persona is commentating in real time on what he/she sees as he/she walks around the village; each of the other personas delivers their stanza in a slightly different form. Miss Maiden's stanza is elliptical and internal, a sequence of thoughts; the Farmer appears to be confiding in someone, perhaps the Vicar; the Vicar seems to be talking to himself, perhaps out loud, and the Librarian is clearly speaking confidentially and directly to the reader.

Themes

Is this a 'model village'? Yes and no. No village could be described as 'model', because every collection of real people inevitably includes a proportion of people with dark secrets. This village is therefore ironically model, in that it is the norm. Where Duffy perhaps parts company from many people is the impression she gives that *all* the inhabitants fall into this category.

The poem shows that people are rarely what they seem; many choose not to share what really goes on in their minds with anyone; others naively don't see below the surface. Casting a child as the main persona is a reminder of another key theme in Duffy's work, which is the alienating voyage from childhood (innocence) to adulthood (experience) — a voyage that a number of Duffy personas, including the Vicar, fail to make successfully.

'Recognition'

This poem is about an old woman and her recognition of how the passing years have diminished her. The shopping trip narrative is interspersed with her observations, leading to cruel juxtapositions, such as when her humiliation at forgetting her purse is placed next to 'I lay in my slip on the wet grass,/laughing'. Note the role of the mirror, a common motif in Duffy's poetry; the recognition is when she realises that the 'anxious, dowdy matron' is her.

'And How Are We Today?'

The persona here is 'inside someone else's head', i.e. schizophrenic. He/she is in a mental institution, as the condescending title implies. The persona enjoys delusions of power but also thinks he/she is at the mercy of the radio, as is suggested by the desperation of 'BASTARDS'. Duffy presents this persona neutrally and leaves the reader to decide on his/her response.

'Psychopath'

A psychopath is someone with a personality disorder that causes him/her to be antisocial, often violent, and to feel no remorse for his/her actions. Robert Hare, a famous expert on psychopathy, defines psychopaths as 'social predators who charm, manipulate and ruthlessly plough their way through life… Completely lacking in conscience and feelings for others, they selfishly take what they want and do as they please, violating social norms and expectations without the slightest sense of guilt or regret'. This description closely fits the persona. Not all psychopaths are murderers, but many are, and in the popular imagination the term is closely associated with serial killers. Duffy deliberately sets out this expectation, and then invites the reader to judge whether it is a fair description. On balance, it is, but the reader may be surprised by hints of, if not sympathy, then at least understanding shown by Duffy. The title arguably leads the reader to expect a monster.

The persona

The persona is an itinerant fairground worker in the early 1960s. The reader is led to feel disgust for him because of his apparent detachment from the crime he has just committed. His desire to be cool is both immature and evidence of his need for approval; his attempts at casual indifference may, however, mask more complicated feelings underneath. He is obsessed with film, several times comparing himself to American film stars, and in places the poem reads like a script for the movie he would like to be starring in, e.g. 'Lamp light. Jimmy Dean'.

The persona's voice is problematic: not only are the vocabulary and grammar often inconsistent with the character; so, at times, are the subtlety of the thought processes. A number of unannounced subject shifts (characteristic of the stream-of-consciousness technique) mean that the reader has to take great care to establish what is being referred to. In stanza 4, for example, 'She' in line 6 is not Dirty Alice, but the victim; this emphasises the interchangeability of women for him.

The emotional state of the persona is perhaps the most chilling aspect of the poem. 'Bang in the centre of my skull,/there's a strange coolness': he shows no remorse for what he has done, and the reader must wonder whether this is the first time he has killed in this way. He is living out a fantasy image of himself, drawn from role models in films, and the reader assumes that his boasts are starkly at variance with the reality. He does not know 'what women want'; the cool confidence of his account does not convince. 'My looks, my luck, my brain': does the reader believe his description of himself?

The opening

The use of the present tense at the beginning of the poem creates an impression of immediacy. After the first sentence, short, ungrammatical phrases reflect an urgent, interior monologue. The stanza is highly visual and reminiscent of a film script

(e.g. 'Lamp light'). It includes non sequiturs and lacks explanation (e.g. 'She is in the canal' doesn't reveal *who* is in the canal). The colloquialisms and references evoke the atmosphere, place and period. The opening image of the persona's reflection posing among dummies may suggest that he is no more human than they are.

The narrative

There is a narrative strand embedded in this poem, plus flashes forward to the end of the narrative, and there are more general observations made by the persona, mostly about himself. Like his mates, the persona likes to impress and pick up 'local girls'. He first saw his victim on the carousel; he bought her a toffee-apple and won a bear for her at a sideshow. They rode on the dodgems, and he won her a goldfish, which she carried in a polythene bag. He persuaded her to walk with him on the towpath by the canal. At this point she had misgivings: '*I'm not that type*, she said'. So he forced her down and raped her: '*No, don't.*' Then he killed her and threw her body in the canal. We do not know her name or age. He is looking back over the events of the evening once he has returned to the town; he checks his reflection in shop windows, perhaps to ensure there is no sign of the struggle, then goes to the pub for a drink.

Women

Among this narrative, the persona hints at two formative experiences in his childhood: with Dirty Alice and seeing his mother with the 'Rent Man'. Indeed, his defective relationship with women lies at the heart of this poem. His first sexual experience was with Dirty Alice when he was 12 years old. He stole the pound she demanded for sexual initiation, so the encounter was as mercenary as it was mechanical. He pulled her knickers down but she merely 'used' him (an important concept, because he now 'uses' the girls he meets) rather than satisfying him. She presumably jeered at him because he was too young, or for some other inadequacy. He despises his mother ('Mama, straight up, I hope you rot in hell'), but we do not know whether her adulterous relationship with the 'Rent Man' is the only reason. The incident is merely sketched in the form of a few significant memories.

Note that his references to both women are directly followed by ones to his victim ('She told me her name', 'She is in the canal'). The ambiguity of the pronouns seems to reflect a suggestion that in killing the girl from the fairground, he is killing by proxy the two women responsible for his earlier disappointments.

The ending

At the end of the poem, the persona appears to be cheerful and optimistic ('I could almost fly'); tomorrow he will move on to a new beginning, although he probably knows that it will be characterised by the same emptiness again: 'the world's your fucking oyster.' He takes refuge in the familiar meaninglessness of a pop song. But there are signs that he is aware that he may not get away with his crime: 'The barman calls Time.' The reference to Ruth Ellis is pointed: she was hanged for murder.

Duffy's sympathies

Although the persona is hardly someone with whom the reader would expect Duffy to have any sympathy, she gives him a sensitivity that is at first surprising. He makes some lyrical observations, e.g. 'These streets are quiet, as if the town has held its breath/to watch the Wheel go round above the dreary homes'. He uses little offensive language; even his violence is mostly suppressed. Phrases such as 'I remember the wasps, the sun blazing', which note the details engraved on the memory in the moment of trauma, are characteristic of Duffy. Despite this, the language changes register alarmingly, from lyricism to obscenity: 'the world's your fucking oyster'. The poem includes many metaphors, such as 'The sky slammed down on my school cap' (compare the ending of 'Stafford Afternoons') — this is a powerful metaphor for the persona's world falling in on him. His boasts and his relationships are empty (does he have any friends? — none are mentioned, and psychopaths are usually loners).

The effect of this is to mute the starkness of the portrait and to make it harder to separate the persona from the poet, although it would be surprising if Duffy identified with him in any conventional way. You might argue that if the psychopath were simply a vile, foul-mouthed monster there would be no purpose in writing the poem.

The persona is part of the group of men who murder, rape, assault and abuse women, a recurring theme for Duffy. His absence of feeling for his victim is only a more extreme form of a common phenomenon; it is not only psychopathic men who abuse women and girls. The persona has characteristics typical of many other male Duffy characters, such as inadequacy, immaturity, lack of empathy and a failure to control his base sexual urges. These failures are rooted in traumatic childhood experiences. The persona is an example of men who live in a fantasy world, in this case imagining himself as a movie star. The poem deals with the theme of what lies beneath the normal exterior, which is also evident in 'Model Village'. Note the importance of the mirror motif, which acts as a reflection of the soul and can represent narcissism as well as self-knowledge. The poem starts with a reflection; in line 15 'My breath wipes me from the looking-glass'; in the final stanza the persona is so far distanced from reality that it is his reflection that 'sucks a sour Woodbine and buys me a drink'. Many of Duffy's characters seek affirmation or self-knowledge through looking at their reflections, as if their grip on reality is otherwise tenuous.

References and allusions

- 'the D.A.', line 1: the duck's arse, a hairstyle common in the 1950s and early 1960s, in which the hair is swept back to a point at the nape of the neck, resembling a duck's tail

- 'Burton's', line 2: a men's clothing shop with mannequins ('dummies') in the window
- 'Jimmy Dean', line 3: James Dean, American film star and rebel idolised by teenage boys; he died aged only 24 in a car crash in 1955
- 'make myself crystal', line 5: i.e. crystal clear
- '*Johnny, Remember Me*', line 7: song by John Leyton, popular in 1961
- 'Brando', line 9: Marlon Brando, another ruggedly handsome American film star, notorious for 'loose living', both on and off screen
- 'the Tunnel of Love', line 12: fairground ride; two people sit together in a car and travel through a dark tunnel, offering opportunities for kissing etc.; could also refer to the vagina
- 'zip up the leather', line 13: he is wearing a leather jacket
- 'looking-glass', line 16: another word for mirror, but also a reminder of *Alice Through the Looking Glass* by Lewis Carroll
- 'handrail to Venus', line 20: rhyming slang for penis
- 'the dodgems', line 21: fairground ride in which people drive around an arena in small electric cars and either dodge the other riders or, more commonly, crash into them; teenage boys could show off in this way when they were too young to drive
- 'frenched it down her throat', line 22: i.e. French-kissed her
- 'Elvis nothing', line 35: an **ellipsis**, meaning Elvis Presley has nothing on me
- 'the Wheel', line 47: fairground ride, the Big Wheel
- 'Woodbine', line 56: type of cheap cigarette
- 'Ruth Ellis', line 59: a notorious murderer, the last woman to be hanged in Britain in 1955
- 'the barman calls Time', line 60: pubs in Britain were required by law to close at 11 p.m.; the barman would call 'Time' when the bar was about to close
- 'A wopbopaloobopalopbimbam', line 63: a meaningless phrase from a popular song, to be sung **rhythmically**

'Selling Manhattan'

This is the title poem of Duffy's second published volume, and you can therefore expect it to indicate some of the central themes of the collection. This is an angry poem. The rape of America by Europeans is a topic of concern to many people. The Native Americans were cheated out of their land where possible, or they were hounded off it by violence. Manhattan Island, now the main part of New York City, was allegedly bought by Dutchman Peter Minuit from its Native American owners for $26 in 1626.

The personas

The poem takes its tone from the mood of the Native American persona. Although Duffy does not specify the persona's gender, she could perhaps be a woman, because symbolically women are raped by men in the same way that the land has been raped; because of the persona's sensitivity; and because the 'loved one' who was killed and 'fell back in [her] arms' was presumably her husband, the warrior, fighting to protect their way of life against the invader. Nevertheless, there is no conclusive evidence (as in many other poems) and the ambiguity is no doubt intended.

Despite what he/she has witnessed, the persona shows resignation and calm acceptance of what has happened. He/she has quiet confidence that the earth and its spirits, in which he/she believes, will exact their own revenge on the usurping white men. He/she has learned wisdom from the horrific experiences he/she has endured, and in any case believes that his/her spirit will live on.

There is a striking contrast between the attitudes of the two personas. The sensitivity of the Native American is juxtaposed with the brutish, selfish, arrogant indifference of the European. The settler is heard only through the 4 lines of the **epigraph**, although we learn a lot about him from the Native American's comments, too. He is a repugnant stereotype and only too aware of the unfairness of the '*bargain*' he has made, and his use of religion — '*Praise the Lord*' — is equally cynical. '*Now get your red ass out of here*' reveals his fundamental racism.

The Native American worships the earth, and his/her response is to appeal to 'the ground' and 'the spirit of the water'. 'I sing with true love for the land' he/she says, and every word of the poem bears this out, as well as his/her capacity for empathy. He/she is acutely aware of the moral inferiority of the Europeans, as 'Man who fears death' reveals. He/she likens the loss of her land to 'a boy [who] feels his freedom vanish', in turn 'like the salmon going mysteriously/out to sea'. He/she reveals her belief in immortality: 'I will live in the ghost of grasshopper and buffalo.' These creatures are also native to America.

Style and form

Compared to the crudity of the settler, whose impoverished vocabulary and **syntax** reflect his atrophied moral sense, the Native American speaks a lyrical poetry. Her diction is sophisticated, and there is a gravity to his/her utterances that matches the seriousness of his/her thoughts: 'I have learned/the solemn laws of joy and sorrow, in the distance/between morning's frost and firefly's flash at night'; 'Loss holds the silence of great stones.' The images of nature, continuity, age and grandeur lend majesty to what he/she says.

After the opening 4 lines of the colonist, the poem is organised into regular 5-line stanzas that are end-stopped, each addressing a particular idea. The final stanza, however, has a line wholly missing, perhaps as a symbol of death and loss.

Themes

Clearly this is a political poem. By juxtaposing the shallow cynicism of the European with the deep wisdom of the Native American, the terrible injustice of colonial conquest is highlighted.

- '*Injun*', line 1: a common way of representing the pronunciation of 'Indian' by non-Native Americans
- '*twenty-four bucks' worth of glass beads*', line 1: a buck is slang for a US dollar
- '*fire-water*', line 3: alcohol, generally whisky, sold or given to Native Americans
- '*red ass*', line 4: native Americans were referred to as 'Red Indians' by Europeans

'Stealing'

This poem presents another inadequate young male persona (see in particular 'Education for Leisure'). The key is that he is bored and purposeless: 'Mostly I'm so bored I could eat myself.' Although this is another monologue, the persona is speaking directly to an audience, and bitterly concludes: 'You don't understand a word I'm saying, do you?'

'The Virgin Punishing the Infant'

Another of the poems based upon a work of art. The painting of the same name by Max Ernst (1891–1976) depicts a mother spanking a naked child across her knees, with what seems to be a halo on the ground, evidently fallen from the child's head. It is similar to a number of poems in *The World's Wife* in which biblical episodes are revisited from a new perspective. The identity of the persona is puzzling until the original picture is seen: a group of people are watching the disturbing scene depicted in the painting through a window. Ernst was a prominent German surrealist painter and poet and a founder-member of the Dada movement.

'Big Sue and *Now, Voyager*'

Now, Voyager is a film made in 1942 starring Bette Davis and Paul Henreid. It has been described as 'the quintessential soap-opera or "woman's picture"' (**www.filmsite.org**). The title is taken from the poem 'Now Finale to the Shore' by the nineteenth-century American poet Walt Whitman: 'Now, Voyager/Sail thou forth to seek and find.' The character played by Bette Davis is overweight and repressed; after therapy with a psychotherapist, she has an affair on board an ocean liner with the married man played by Paul Henreid.

Unusually, this poem is not a monologue by Sue; it is an account of Sue given by a third party, presumably Duffy herself. The poem is also unusual in that the inadequate character rather unsympathetically depicted by Duffy is a woman. Sue is overweight and lives alone in a small flat in Tooting, a London suburb. She avoids facing up to the reality of her situation by retreating into a fantasy world in which she constantly imagines herself to be the Bette Davis character in *Now, Voyager*. This can never bring her any real satisfaction; she may be able to 'press the rewind' in order to 'know perfection' and 'Certainty', but she is bitterly aware that 'Outside the window…slender women rush to meet their dates'. When she cries for the romantic vision enshrined in the film, she is of course crying for her own situation.

The first two stanzas constitute an extended metaphor. Every action Sue makes is identified with *Now, Voyager*. The curtains shut out reality, and Sue lives 'the wrong side of the glass/in black-and-white'. When she believes herself to be unlovable she takes refuge in the fantasy that Paul Henreid, the star of the film, loves her, when in reality his character loves the Bette Davis character, a situation doubly removed from reality because the film is in any case fiction. (Note the juxtaposition of '*Be honest. Who'd love me?*/Paul Henreid': she appears to be answering her own rhetorical question by immediately naming Paul Henreid, although grammatically the reference belongs to the next stanza, which describes the film. Duffy often employs such ambiguity across stanza divides.) When Davis draws on a cigarette, Sue pretends to draw on a chocolate stick (note all the references to food, a substitute for love). 'The little flat in Tooting/is a floating ship', and it constitutes an archetypal voyage of escape for Sue from the reality of her life. 'The precious video unspools the sea' to make this possible.

Although this behaviour harms no one but Sue herself, it could be argued that Duffy implicitly criticises Sue's self-indulgence and failure to take any real action to improve her predicament. The key lines of the film — '*Why wish for the moon?...We have the stars*' — could show an admirable acceptance of reality, but actually emphasise Sue's refusal to take action to solve her problem. Duffy cannot avoid comparing Sue's unreal world behind the curtains and behind the screen with the reality of the world outside, or suggesting that Sue would rather be one of the 'slender women' who are being dated by real men, not by images. However, Duffy may have some sympathy for Sue, and makes no attempt to change her: there is recognition that, for better for worse, this is how she is. The desperately sad tone of the poem arouses sympathy in the reader, as does the irony that Sue doesn't truly believe the message of the film.

The use of italics in this poem is ambiguous. Italics in a Duffy poem usually signify spoken words, in contrast to the unspoken monologue that forms the main body of the poem (note that the reverse is true of 'Model Village'). In this case the use is more complex:

- '*Be honest. Who'd love me?*' (line 6) — these are words semi-spoken by Big Sue, about herself, as if to an interlocutor.
- '*Now, Voyager, depart…*' (lines 10–11) — these words are actually spoken in the film, along with '*Why wish for the moon?*' (line 19) and '*We have the stars*' (line 24).
- '*Size of her. Great cow*' (line 16) — these words are actually (or supposedly?) spoken about Sue by other people.

These words are all, of course, of a different provenance, or in a different voice, from that of the narrator. This device allows Duffy to introduce alternative voices in order to give greater depth to the characterisation.

Style and form

The third person narrator enjoys an omniscient viewpoint and is capable of seeing inside Sue's head, which gives rise to effects similar to those created by the monologue personas that are more characteristic of Duffy's poems. It is as if Duffy, much of the time, is writing what is passing through Sue's mind.

The vocabulary is not sophisticated: the sentences are mostly short and are often ungrammatical, reflecting both Sue's presumably limited education and the typical level of Hollywood movies (although, actually, the language of the film has an elevated tone typical of its period; note the romantic diction and ordering of the utterance '*Now, Voyager, depart. Much,/much for thee is yet in store*', which is in fact a quotation from the Whitman poem upon which the film is to some extent based). There is a regular juxtaposition of Sue's self-indulgent fantasy with the real world outside, and the language used to describe the latter tends to be more fluent and subtle, e.g. 'Men whistle/on the dark blue streets at shapes they want'.

Themes

The themes of the poem include inadequacy, self-indulgence, the contrast between fantasy and reality, loneliness and the outsider. The obsession with movies (or a particular movie) is a recurring theme, image or motif in Duffy's poetry. Sue has retreated entirely into a fantasy that prevents her from making a realistic assessment of her situation and taking action to alleviate it. So long as she can pretend that Paul Henreid loves her as she is, she does not need to curb her appetites. Ironically, for a film about sailing away into a new and wider world, Sue's horizons are cruelly limited. '*Much,/much for thee is yet in store*': nothing else is in store for Sue.

'Foreign'

This poem's themes are alienation and language. The persona, an immigrant, still feels an outsider after 20 years: 'this is not home'. The poem is a monologue, but the persona (of indeterminate gender) invites the audience to share the immigrant's perspective by repeatedly saying 'Imagine…'.

'Correspondents'

This is a heterosexual love poem. The monologue is addressed to the beloved but it is clear that he cannot hear it. The tone is wistful and passionate by turns. The precision with which the persona plots the meeting, down to the tiniest detail, shows the depth of her feeling, but perhaps suggests a touch of obsession.

'Telegrams'

The poem takes the form of an epistolary dialogue in telegrams, which are capitalised because that is how telegrams were written. Since there was no punctuation on early teleprinters, the convention was that 'STOP' had to be placed wherever a full stop would have been used — which permits the final repetition. The theme is the betrayal of the woman by an untrustworthy man, who turns out to have been concealing the existence of his wife from his lover, but it is possible the woman does not regret the end of the relationship — 'thought it odd you wore string vest' is a surprisingly humorous comment in the circumstances.

'Lovesick'

This is a whimsical poem: the apple is a metaphor for the love the persona has found, which she keeps hidden away 'in the attic' for fear that someone will destroy it — 'You with the big teeth'.

'Warming Her Pearls'

Judith Radstone, to whom the poem is dedicated, was a politically radical bookseller. The connexion with Duffy is explained in an obituary published after her death in 2001: 'Carol Ann Duffy's "Warming Her Pearls" was dedicated to Judith, inspired by a conversation with her about the practice of ladies' maids increasing the lustre of their mistresses' pearls by secreting them beneath their clothes to be warmed by their skin.' There is a subtly erotic overtone to Duffy's working of this idea; the maid is fascinated by her mistress, and derives pleasure from the idea of the pearls which she has warmed lying upon her mistress's skin. Pearls are symbols of inaccessible treasure, and of female genitalia.

'Miles Away'

This delightful love poem includes a metaphorical description of the condensation of breath on cold night air: 'breathing the colour thought is/before language into still air.' Duffy's fascination with film reappears: 'The stars are filming us for no one.'

From *The Other Country* (1990)

'Originally'

This is another poem about the alienation of emigration, which it universalises with the memorable line: 'All childhood is an emigration.' Note the echo of '*I want our own country*' in the very different 'My country./I want it back' of 'The Captain of the 1964 *Top of the Form* Team'. This persona has made the transition from childhood to adulthood successfully (in contrast with 'Foreign'): 'my voice/in the classroom sounding just like the rest.' A 'skelf' is an old Celtic word for a splinter.

'In Mrs Tilscher's Class'

Nostalgia for schooldays appears again in this poem. A key term of transition is remembered by the persona: as the tadpoles mutated into frogs, so she changed

from a child to a young adult, the thunderstorm at end of the poem representing the onset of puberty. 'This was better than home': the excitement of education and a new world opening up to an eager young mind is symbolised by the exotic 'Blue Nile'. 'Brady and Hindley' are a reminder of the dark world that awaits beyond the gates of the school: Ian Brady and Myra Hindley were the notorious 'Moors Murderers' who killed a number of children in the mid-1960s and buried their bodies on the Lancashire Moors.

'Weasel Words'

Background

The epigraph refers to Sir Robert Armstrong, who was cabinet secretary between 1979 and 1987, when Margaret Thatcher was prime minister. The statement is extraordinary and carefully phrased: under what conceivable circumstances could it have been 'explained' to the cabinet secretary, the head of the Civil Service, what '*weasel words*' meant? The answer gives the context of the poem, without which it cannot be understood.

In 1986 Peter Wright, a former senior officer of MI5 (the British Secret Service), attempted to publish a book entitled *Spycatcher*, in which he alleged a number of scandals about the service. Thatcher was furious, and attempted to block the book's publication. In Australia, this attempt at censorship was tested in a momentous court case. Armstrong represented the British government and tried to persuade the court that the book should not be published. Under intense cross-questioning, Armstrong was forced to admit that he had been 'economical with the truth', a phrase which then entered the English language. He was also accused of having used 'weasel words'. The outcome of the trial was sensational: the judge refused to grant the British government's wishes and *Spycatcher* was duly published, initially in Australia and subsequently worldwide, to the considerable embarrassment of the government.

The metaphor

This is a dense, difficult and important poem. The speaker is a member of the Weasel political party delivering a speech in the House of Commons. In the House of Commons, government MPs sit on one side and opposition MPs sit on the other. The words in italics show that the poem is represented as if it were an entry in *Hansard*, the official record of parliamentary debates; the other members of the house are allowed to say '*Hear, hear*' when they agree with the point being made, and such interjections are recorded in italics. The Ferrets are clearly the opposing political party.

The metaphor works on a number of levels, and it is important to distinguish between them. At the first level, it is a parody of the House of Commons. But this is a House of Commons for the animal world: are the two opposing parties literally weasels and ferrets, or are these merely metaphorical labels for human parties? This ambiguity is maintained throughout, because the content of the speech is also explicitly animal but could equally be seen as a metaphor for humans. This is a polished piece of parliamentary rhetoric; politicians speak to persuade, without any particular concern for the truth, which is what the Weasel speaker does. But the important matter is that, try as he might, the speaker only reinforces more clearly that, in actuality, the Weasels and Ferrets are indistinguishable — both are 'long, slim-bodied carnivores'. His admission, near the end, that 'Our brown fur coats turn white in winter' clearly reveals that appearances cannot be trusted. Here the metaphor for politicians is unmistakable: that they are all the same, that they 'turn their coats' as the situation demands. The final half-stanza is ambiguous: is the speaker really demonstrating the sucking-out of an egg? This surprises the reader, since it gives ammunition to a critic about the hollowness of his words. Perhaps this is another case of Duffy's voice subtly taking over and turning the poem to her own ends, to display the truth behind the words, or perhaps the weasel lacks self-control and gives way to his animal instincts.

Having arrived at the end, it is possible to go full circle and return to the **epigraph**. This, surely, is what led Duffy to write the poem in the first place: to actualise the metaphor about 'weasel words', and to extend it to the whole breed of politicians being identifiable with weasels; the metaphor of the sucked egg is actualised in the final two lines, and reminds us of the slaughter of the innocents.

It is hard not to read this poem in a smooth, superior, arrogant tone. The Weasels are the natural party of power and represent the political elite; they are highly educated and supremely confident. The Weasel is smug and sinister and there is a tone of menace, e.g. 'Pure bias/on the part of your Natural History Book'; 'You can trust a Weasel'.

Given the explicit reference to Thatcher's Conservative government, it is reasonable to assume that the Weasels can be identified with the Conservatives. The Ferrets would therefore be the Labour Party, the party of opposition — ferret-keeping is a predominantly working-class hobby.

Style and form

This poem is a spoken monologue aimed at an audience (and includes its interjections). It is therefore not written in a **'stream of consciousness'** style, unlike so many of Duffy's other poems. It uses formal, grammatical English; its elevated language and syntax imitate the style and register of a Commons speech. The speaker employs humour ('put a Weasel/down his trouser leg', 'Pure bias/on the part of your Natural History Book') and **satirises** the ferrets in various ways.

Evidence of the rhetorical diction of the weasel speaker is easy to find: 'this is absolutely not the case'; 'exceptionally/short legs'; 'we have never denied this';

'Furthermore'; 'let me continue'. These persuasive devices are examples of **periphrasis** and **litotes**, beloved of politicians.

Themes

It could be argued that the poem is about appearance and reality. Weasel words appear to have meaning but are in reality empty. The egg sucked out by the Weasel in the final stanza appears to be 'A whole egg' but is merely a hollow shell — as, Duffy might argue, is the case with politics as a whole, or perhaps with the Conservative party as a whole. 'Our brown fur coats turn white in winter' certainly conveys the idea that appearances can be deceptive, and there is a suggestion of 'turncoat' — a traitor.

References and allusions

- weasel: a small mammal with a long body, similar in appearance to a ferret. It eats meat, sucks eggs, and is generally considered to be unpleasant. Also used to refer to a sly or treacherous person.
- 'Hear, hear', line 4: traditional way of expressing agreement in the House of Commons
- 'put a Weasel/down his trouser-leg', lines 7–8: a ferret put down a man's trousers is likely to administer a painful bite; competitions were allegedly held in the north of England in which men displayed their endurance by submitting to this risk
- 'a Weasel/does not break the spinal cord of its victim with one bite', lines 10–11 — ferrets can and do

'Poet for Our Times'

This monologue is delivered at a bar, as the interjections such as 'cheers' and 'my shout' testify. The poem illustrates Duffy's interest in the media, in this case the tabloid press. The examples of headlines (given in capitals) show both the elliptical and often ambiguous style typically employed (e.g. CECIL–KEAYS ROW SHOCK TELLS EYETIE WAITER' is a highly condensed version of 'Italian waiter reports the shocking story of Cecil Parkinson and Sarah Keays having a public row in the restaurant in which he works'), but also the set of prejudices embodied in such papers: nationalism ('EYETIE', for an Italian; 'FROG', for a French person); obsession with sex scandals ('PANTIE ROMP', 'BONKING SHOCK'); the crude, overt sexism of using naked women to sell newspapers ('SEE PAGE 3 TODAY GENTS THEY'RE GIGANTIC' — 'they' being the exposed breasts of a young woman).

Duffy's disgust at this male camaraderie is apparent, but she puts a revealing thought into the persona's mind: that tabloid headlines are 'the poems of the decade', and the final line is a turning of the phrase 'tits and bums' (the obsession of the male-dominated tabloid press) into 'bottom line', i.e. the only things that really matter are bottoms and profits. Whether it is 'art', however (the closing word), is the important question which Duffy poses.

'Making Money'

This poem is about obsession with making money at any cost, including injury or death in the developing world. Duffy associates this with Thatcher and the 1980s. The catalogue of alternative names for money is a characteristic Duffy device. Although the poem is a monologue, the character of the persona does not come across particularly clearly until the final stanza, when Duffy slips into lyrical mood, as if to suggest that the people taken over by greed once had souls and sensitivity.

'Descendants'

Told from the perspective of an ignorant, illiterate, alcoholic male thug, this is an example of how Duffy uses the words of her personas to damn themselves in the eyes of the reader. The persona's vocabulary is as impoverished as his moral sense, e.g. 'knackered', 'Big fucking deal'. The reader wonders how he came to have the girlfriend Sarah, who is not only able to read, but actually enjoyed the volume of poetry passed down by her grandmother. The title is of course ironic: the book will not be passed down to *their* descendants, because he has thrown it into the sea and then wonders why she is crying.

'Liar'

Another inadequate persona is described, although this time not through her own monologue but in a rare third-person narration, i.e. the voice is Duffy's. Note a number of familiar motifs, such as the mirror and the sustained comparison with film. The narrative is elliptical: it reveals glimpses of all the contexts in which the character lies, and then, in a contemporary social comment, she attempts to abduct a child, claiming it as hers (a neurosis of 1990s Britain — see *Waterland* by Graham Swift and *The Child in Time* by Ian McEwan). The 'experts' pigeonhole her, but the 'top psychiatrist' has problems of his own (the reader has to imagine 'what he does every night to the Princess of Wales', i.e. Princess Diana). Duffy evenhandedly describes the weaknesses of the unfortunate (the persona) and of the elite (the 'top psychiatrist').

'Boy'

A clear echo of the Vicar in 'Model Village', this poem presents another man psycho-sexually arrested in boyhood and returning there in fantasy, although this takes a slightly different form. Needless to say, the persona in 'Boy' is socially inadequate and is forced to resort to the 'Lonely Hearts' column in the newspaper to find friendship. His calling the elder woman '*Mummy*' gives a hint at the cause of his failure to mature.

'Eley's Bullet'

This poem is based upon the coincidence that Eley, the protagonist of the poem, shares his name with a well-known make of shotgun cartridge. It is a sad tale of the forlorn love of the farmer Eley and a married woman from the town.

'Dream of a Lost Friend'

Another view of disappointed love, this time because the loved one is dead but comes back in a disorientating dream. Although there is some direct evidence of the gender of the loved one, 'a child-man's laugh', and none about the gender of the persona, the poem is clearly about AIDS (the 'virus' nurtured by 'Some of our best friends', literally in this case although often for Duffy a metaphor) and the death of a male homosexual lover. In the mid-1990s, the time when the poem was written, the treatments for AIDS were ineffective and thousands of otherwise fit young men died.

'Who Loves You'

A meditation on an absent loved one, again of indeterminate gender. The persona is worrying about the safety of the beloved, who seems to have been sent to a dangerous, faraway place.

'Girlfriends'

A poem about lesbian passion.

'Words, Wide Night'

A poem about a distant loved one.

'River'

This is an important poem because it deals with so many of Duffy's central concerns: language and its nature, distance and alienation, identity, reality and imagination, concrete and metaphorical, familiar and foreign, as well as multiplicity of viewpoints.

The question of viewpoint is especially difficult. There is no real persona, in the usual sense, in this poem; it appears to be a meditation by the poet, initially in the form of a present-tense report of what she witnesses, and then in the form of a direct engagement with the reader, addressed as 'you'. On the first level, the persona/poet appears to be travelling down a physical river, perhaps on a slow boat, and notes that, as the river crosses a frontier, it does not change at all, but the land through which it runs is changed. This is, of course, an oblique comment upon the arbitrary nature of human frontiers and divisions. Humans create artificial distinctions, for example by giving different names to the same river (e.g. Duna, Donau, Danube), but to nature its unity is self-evident. Hence the ability of water to 'translate itself', which the humans cannot match, and the sign 'in new language' is brash both because it intrudes upon nature, and because it is suddenly out of keeping with what has gone before.

The persona appears to be travelling along a river, although there is no indication of how. There is no mention of anybody else, as there might be if he/she were on a boat; in fact, there is an air of unreality about the whole thing, because the woman on the bank seems completely unaware of the persona passing. And yet it seems to be a concrete situation: there is considerable detail about the setting, the bird and the woman. The complete absence of practical detail about the observer reinforces the suspicion that, despite the present-tense observations, the observer is not 'really' there and this is not 'really' happening.

After the first two stanzas there is an abrupt transition of style and mood, and the narrator/observer/persona addresses the reader directly: 'What would it mean to you if you could be/with her there'. 'She' must be the woman who is introduced in line 7, and who proves to be a central concern of the poem. The viewpoint moves swiftly in the third stanza: from the poet to 'you', inviting the reader to identify so fully with the scene that 'you' are 'dangling your own hands in the water', and then shifting again to the woman, confidently imagining how she feels, and why. It is just possible that the woman really is singing a nonsense rhyme, because she is happy; if so, this reinforces that view that the poet/observer, if she is 'really' there, is not perceptible to the woman. Far more likely, though, is that the woman is singing in her own language, which sounds like nonsense to the observer. It is also possible that she is imitating the bird's song.

The poem is, of course, another example of the actualisation of metaphor of which Duffy is so fond. While the first level of reading sees a real river, the river can also be seen as a metaphor for the river of life down which we are all carried, like the poet, helplessly, observing what happens on the banks as we pass, and often taking us into bewilderingly new countries. Following this metaphor to its conclusion, when 'the river runs into the sea' we must assume this means the point of death, so the question 'what would you write on a postcard,/or on the sand…?' becomes all the more poignant.

Arguably, the metaphorical river becomes more important than the physical river, which helps us to make sense of the concluding lines. If 'you' were really at the end of the metaphorical river of life, what message would you leave? This is Duffy's invitation to the reader to respond to the ideas she has suggested.

Style and form

This is one of Duffy's most lyrical poems. The writing has a limpid clarity that is mimetic of the gentle flow of the river. The register is elevated and the syntax is complex to reflect the range of ideas alluded to or included. The sentences run sinuously, flowing and slipping away; the incidence of commas is high, allowing the poet to run ideas past the reader in the same, continuous way that objects appear and pass on the bank of the river. There are many sibilants and some **alliteration**.

Themes

There are repeated references to language, starting with the first line, as well as 'words stumble', the sign being 'in new language', and the woman asking for the

name of the bird. In the third stanza, the 'blue and silver fish' dart away and, 'like the meanings of things', vanish, an image that illustrates the way language shifts: 'stone,/stoon, stein'. The woman is 'somewhere else' 'because/of words'. The invitation to the reader in the closing two lines is to record — in words, but in which language? — his/her response. Duffy may be suggesting that language runs through life, constantly changing, but is a central part of experience, like the river; meaning can elude you, but that in the end it is all you have with which to express thoughts and feelings.

'The Way My Mother Speaks'

A personal meditation upon the poet's mother and her pet phrases; it contains the memorable image 'like a child/who stood at the end of summer/and dipped a net/in a green, erotic pond', another example of Duffy's interest in the transition from childhood to adolescence (see also 'Litany', 'Stafford Afternoons', 'In Mrs Tilcher's Class').

'In Your Mind'

This poem can be viewed as the 'title poem' of the collection *The Other Country*, because the phrase forms its opening words. The title emphasises a recurring theme of Duffy's poetry: characters who live more vividly through imagination and fantasy than they do in the real world. The phrase 'the other country' alludes to various similar phrases. L. P. Hartley wrote in *The Go-Between*, 'The past is a foreign country: they do things differently there'; Christopher Marlowe wrote in *The Jew of Malta*, 'But that was another country'; *Another Country* is a play (and film) by Julian Mitchell about an individual betraying his homeland in favour of an adopted country.

The persona

There is little evidence as to the gender of the persona. This is a rare example of a Duffy poem set in the workplace, from which the persona is so desperate to escape that he/she daydreams away the afternoon. It is also unusual in its use of 'you'. There is no indication that this monologue is actually delivered to an audience; rather, the persona is invoking an imaginary audience (i.e. the reader) to share in the feelings evoked by the 'other country'. There is an ambiguity throughout the poem as to whether the persona is actually addressing the 'you' or whether he/she is using it in the sense of 'one', to universalise it and to invite the audience to share the persona's experiences.

The other country

The poem starts abruptly. As occurs so often in Duffy's poems, 'In Your Mind' starts in the middle of a thought process, leaving the reader to reconstruct the situation from the clues given. The use of 'the' implies that this is a topic to which the persona is returning, suggesting that this is a continuation of a conversation that has perhaps taken place many times with the same interlocutor, the 'you' to whom it is addressed. If the persona had said 'Another country' the force of the reference would have been lost: 'the' requires familiarity, and the idea that it is shared with the reader. It also universalises it: does everyone have a country to which they dream of escaping? Is it real or imaginary? Have they ever been there? The phrase 'half-remembered' suggests that perhaps the 'you' visited it when young, or even has a half-memory from another life.

The phrase '*Of course*' (line 15) is a key point in the poem. It may suggest that the 'other country' is half-remembered because it is (also, or in part) the country of childhood, lost and unattainable but familiar. The italics indicate that this is an utterance in the daydream: it is the point of recognition. The painting has been lost for 30 years since it was last seen in childhood. Another key point is reached with 'knowing its name' (line 23). This could be childhood, the past, home, heaven or whatever it is that has true significance for the persona. The poem invites readers to ask what place or idea would have the same significance for them.

The phrase 'You know people there' develops this idea. The persona has imagined this place so often that he/she has peopled it with characters that have become familiar — they are part of an elaborated fantasy life. The place appears to be in the Mediterranean somewhere — a familiar enough escape for British people seeking physical and human warmth. But the 'other country' differs from the mundane reality of a grey British day in more than climate. 'You swap a coin for a fish' (line 18) suggests the adoption (if only in the imagination) of a simpler, more authentic life, symbolised by this exchange of money (and all its trappings) for all the fish suggests: the outdoors life, good food, the seaside.

In the final stanza, the fantasy has achieved its goal: the persona is fully immersed, 'lost but not lost'. The language is limpid, relaxed and hanging in the warm air, e.g. 'dawdling on the blue bridge'. The six swans passing under the bridge may be a reminder of the fairy tale by the Brothers Grimm, in which they represent lost children. The mood is then suddenly broken, and the flowing sentences are interrupted by a series of blunt, sharp images as reality comes flooding back and the moment is lost.

Style and form

The poem is narrated in the present tense, which creates a sense of the immediacy of a daydream. Parts of the poem are written in long, flowing and elegant sentences, but as the action develops there are non-grammatical words and phrases that describe images and feelings. There is a gentleness and a resignation in the mood of the poem, along with the familiarity of a fantasy lived out many times. Although it ends in disappointment, there is no sense of bitterness, perhaps because it has served its purpose, or because the persona knows he/she will revisit

it soon. The mention of 'a beautiful boy' may hint at frustration in the persona's day-to-day life, or may just be part of the image of a Mediterranean bar. The persona seems content to drift with the images as they occur, not seeking to intervene or shape them.

Themes

These include escape; fantasy; the suggestion that for everyone there is another country that is more real or significant than the one in which they live. It can be both a physical country or a metaphorical one (such as the past or the future).

From *Mean Time* (1993)

'The Captain of the 1964 *Top of the Form* Team'

This is another poem about the inadequacy of men and their inability to grow up. The narrator experienced one moment of (rather trivial) fame and is unable to cope with the failure of the rest of his life to live up to this moment. He is bitter and self-obsessed: he has no relationship with his 'stale' wife or his 'thick' kids, but never reflects upon whether this may be his fault. Although he was 'The Captain' as a child, he is now a mere employee, and has to impress his 'boss' in the pub. He does not reflect upon anything, but obsessively relives his moment of glory and transfers it into the present by inflicting trivia quiz questions upon those around him. His political views are as fixed in the past and as unrealistic as what he says about himself.

Background

Once again, Duffy makes no concessions to her readers, for example by decoding any of the contemporary references (although she does, at least, anchor the poem firmly in a specific historical milieu — Britain, October 1964). The year 1964 was a turning point in British history: a radical Labour government was elected after 13 years of Conservative rule, and social change was in the air, of which The Beatles were a powerful symbol.

Top of the Form was a team quiz show for students aged 14–16 that was broadcast on British television in the 1960s. Although a number of schools submitted teams, only the best were picked to appear on television; the most knowledgeable pupils were chosen for the team, and the captain would be especially bright.

In the 1960s able pupils were selected to attend single-sex grammar schools, while the less intelligent went to mixed secondary moderns (see The 1960s, pp. 12–14). The persona clearly went to a grammar school (where Latin was taught) and bought a new leather satchel by his proud parents as a reward for his achievement. Grammar schools stressed learning by heart, the skill at which the persona excelled, but the world moved on and new skills were needed in order to succeed in the workplace. The persona probably has an insignificant job in a small company (where he can go to the pub for a drink with his 'boss'). Because grammar schools were all single sex, normal social contact with the opposite sex was difficult (the persona hoped to impress the girls from the local convent school but there is no evidence to suggest that he succeeded).

The persona

The poem is probably an internal monologue, as there is no explicit reference to a listener; the use of the second person ('I can give you the B-side') may indicate that this is what he *would* say if he had anybody to talk to. It is possible that he is actually talking (probably in the pub?) to some hapless victim who is given no opportunity to respond to this one-sided torrent of self-congratulation and self-pity. (Compare 'Poet for Our Times', a similar pub monologue, but in that case with a real audience.)

The poem starts in the middle of the monologue, as is suggested by the reference to 'that month', which creates a sense of immediacy but makes the reader work to understand the context (without the title, it would be virtually impossible). The list of song titles, a typical Duffy device, establishes the historical context, and the persona's over-eagerness to provide unwanted information gives the reader an immediate impression of his character.

'*Sir!... Correct*' is a reminder of what the persona wants back: the seal of approval from the adult, not for being intelligent, but for simply regurgitating meaningless facts which he has learned by heart; but it gained him the praise he craved (and which he can no longer attain). The revealing phrase 'for a year' shows that his mother kept his mascot on the television for a while, but then presumably decided that enough was enough. Unfortunately, the persona refused to move on to adult things. Perhaps this fleeting hint at his relationship with his mother (there is no mention of his father at all) gives some indication of the reason for his failure to grow up. The reader is left to flesh out, with his/her imagination, what it must be like living with such an arrogant and inadequate person. His wife is no doubt fed up of his permanently living in the past rather than facing up to his failure in the present; his children no doubt have better things to do than learning general knowledge answers that are of no interest to them.

'My country'

Although the poem begins as a simple showing-off of the persona's knowledge, and a reliving of his moment of childhood fame, the transition from the third to the fourth stanza introduces a new dimension: 'My country./I want it back.' 'My country' sums up all that he had, and has lost. It is the pivot phrase: it refers backwards to the earlier part of the poem and of his life, and forwards, to the final stanza and the present day. It is ambiguous: it refers, first, to the countryside over which, as a boy, he walked, and to his lost glory, when he was 'the one with all the answers'; and then to Britain. He wants the old Britain back (the Britain of Churchill

Way and Nelson Drive). It is a kind of totem to which the persona clings. Because everything about his present life is unsatisfactory to him, he lives in the past, when he knew what his 'country' was and when he seemed to be successful and to have a future before him.

His clinging to his country can be seen in the light of his pride in the valiant achievements of Nelson and Churchill in defending Britain against the attacks of the French and Germans respectively; the irony is that Britain, by joining the European Union, could be seen, by 'little Englanders' like the persona, as having surrendered its sovereignty to the old European foes. His final question — 'How many florins in a pound?' — is doubly nationalistic: not only is he in danger of losing the pound to the euro, but the florin has already vanished with the (Europe-inspired) transition to decimal coinage in 1971. The previous question, about the prime minister of Rhodesia, is both dated (Rhodesia became independent as Zimbabwe in 1980) and politically right wing, because Ian Smith, the prime minister in question, was a noted white supremacist who opposed democracy for the Africans in his country.

'My country' also echoes what is sometimes regarded as a nationalistic hymn, 'I Vow to Thee My Country', and the ultra-nationalistic phrase 'My country, right or wrong'.

Responses to the persona

'*How can we know the dancer from the dance?*' (line 20) is the last line of W. B. Yeats's poem 'Among School Children'. The question is completely out of place and shocks the reader. It is possible that the persona is simply asking the name of the poet who wrote the line, but all the other questions in the poem seem to be in the form in which they were asked in the original television quiz. This is of a wholly different order and poses philosophical questions about the nature of art and existence that, of course, cannot be responded to with a quiz-type answer. This could be a case of Duffy suddenly subverting her character with her own voice or hinting that the persona once was actually intelligent, and asked real questions, before he failed to grow up.

The poem ends with a question, left hanging like so many others, but it embodies both the persona's living in the past (there have been no florins since 1971) and his unease with the cause of the change — the relentless march of European unity, and what he sees as the destruction of the traditional symbols of 'my country'. There is no one to answer his questions, either because they cannot, or they do not care.

It is possible to feel some sympathy with the persona, however. The education system of the 1960s gave the false impression — reinforced by programmes such as *Top of the Form* — that learning facts was enough to be successful.

Style and form

Duffy frequently divides her poems into stanzas, and often uses the stanza-transition for a variety of effects. In this case, the verbal echoes link the stanzas, e.g. 'a two-hour snog./No snags', 'dominus domine dominum/Dave Dee Dozy' are alliterative echoes; in the latter example, both are lists — Latin and pop music respectively.

This poem is written in one of Duffy's characteristic styles — the ungrammatical, reflective, stream-of-consciousness catalogue. Examples of this style include:

- 'fizzing hope. Gargling/with Vimto', lines 5–6: the persona was as bubbly as the soft drink he drank
- 'The clever smell of my satchel', line 6: this is a transferred epithet. It was the owner who was clever, not the satchel, but the satchel signifies cleverness.
- 'Convent girls', line 6: this allusion carries several ideas — the persona deluded himself that convent girls would be attracted to him because he was clever. Girls who attended a religious, off-limits school for girls were a typical fantasy for boys of the time, especially those attending single-sex grammar schools. They were virgins, unattainable, and yet (he implies) they were interested in him.
- 'the white sleeve/of my shirt saluted', lines 12–13: this is a striking metaphor; as the persona puts up his hand in class to answer the teacher's questions, it looks like an arm raised in salute — a Nazi salute, which we later see to be appropriate
- 'no hands, famous, learning', line 16: this is his image of himself — daring and cool because he is riding his bicycle with no hands; famous because he has appeared on television at a time when to do so was much more uncommon for an ordinary person than it is now; learning because that is what he was always doing, even if he was only learning trivia
- 'I look/so brainy you'd think I'd just had a bath', lines 18–19: how 1960s! This refers to the middle-class association of cleanliness with academic attainment and of mere learning with braininess.

Themes

The themes include nostalgia and obsession with the past; self-obsession and lack of self-knowledge; immature fantasy and self-image; politics (unreflective, nationalistic right-wing views).

References and allusions

- music references, lines 1–3: '*Do Wah Diddy Diddy*' is by Manfred Mann; '*Baby Love*' is by the Supremes; '*Oh Pretty Woman*' is by Roy Orbison; 'I can give you the B-side' refers to the 45-rpm vinyl singles of which the 'Top Ten' was composed in 1964 — they had an A-side, which was the song that people bought, and another, less well-known song on the reverse, which was the B-side
- 'Vimto', line 6: a sweet, fizzy drink, dark in colour to give the impression that it is wine
- 'I blew like Mick', line 8: Mick Jagger, lead singer of the pop group The Rolling Stones, famously used to pout; the narrator uses his comb to emulate this facial expression

- 'Dyke Hill', line 15: a curious name — all the street names in the poem are significant, so this could be a snide reference to lesbianism; it would be in keeping with the persona's political philosophy for him to be prejudiced against such people
- '*dominus domine dominum*', line 16: in grammar schools the study of Latin was compulsory, and it involved learning by heart the declension of nouns; the persona is reciting one of these
- 'Dave Dee Dozy', line 17: another 1960s pop group (in full, Dave Dee, Dozy, Beaky, Mick and Titch)
- 'Gonk', line 17: a stuffed toy often used as a lucky mascot
- '*A Hard Day's Night*', line 19: a song by The Beatles that begins with a single distinctive guitar chord
- '*Bzz*', line 25: the sound made by the buzzer in the television programme *Top of the Form* when the contestants signalled they knew an answer
- '*How many florins in a pound?*', line 32: a florin was a two-shilling piece, worth the equivalent of 10 pence in decimal currency

'Litany'

A litany is a form of prayer that consists of a series of invocations, each followed by an unvarying response, or a long or tedious speech or recital. This double meaning of unquestioning devotion and monotony is certainly applicable to the poem. The meeting of housewives to buy items from a catalogue, a popular activity in the 1960s, could be viewed as the secular equivalent of a church service: it has a similar formality, set of shared expectations and reverence of tone, and it includes a kind of litany — a list of the items for sale. This could be seen as an equation of consumerism with religion (compare with Philip Larkin, especially *The Whitsun Weddings*).

The persona

The persona is a young girl — perhaps aged 12 or 13 — at the time the events took place, although here, as in many other poems, the evidence is deliberately inconclusive and the reader must form his/her own judgement. It was a memorable age for her, because she remembers other events of that year. She is young enough for the use of the sexual expletive by the boy to have been shocking and new, and old enough to know exactly the response that her repeating of it would have on the gathering. The poem hints at her relationship with her mother: she sat at her feet, pretending to read, actually following intently what was going on. She knew that it was important to her mother's self-esteem to be a successful host of such a party, that her house and standards were under scrutiny, and it is a sign of a childish cruelty to prick the bubble of middle-class pretentiousness in this way. The persona's shrewd but biting comments on the gathering are, of course, spoken with hindsight, so in this case there is no inconsistency in the persona's observations. (How many of them did she feel at the time? The reader is left to infer.)

Mood and atmosphere

The mood of the gathering is tense and brittle. At that time, many middle-class women felt an extreme need to conform to the expectations of their peers. The host feels that she is being watched and judged at every moment, and dare not make a mistake in the proceedings of the meeting (e.g. 'The Lounge/would seem to bristle with eyes'). The persona suggests that all the women were victims of 'terrible marriages' – that they were treated unequally by their husbands and relegated to a position of inferiority epitomised by their attendance at this event. The persona suggests that the tension was palpable, like the crackling of electricity in the air. Note that the man of the house — the persona's father — is never referred to. The metaphor gains its force because both elements — cellophane and polyester — are new, artificial materials, which both make an audible crackling sound, and also generate static electricity which creates tension and can lead to a physical 'bristle', although of hair not eyes. The man-made nature of these materials also emphasises the unnatural atmosphere in the room.

In a middle-class home the lounge was viewed as a kind of holy place; family members were not normally allowed to enter it because it was reserved for visitors and formal occasions — again, like a church. The capitalisation reinforces this impression of it being a sanctified rather than homely place. The persona observes 'No one had cancer, or sex, or debts': the stereotype, which had to be lived up to, was that everything was fine; no failure, weakness or ill-health could be admitted to. Duffy suggests that this false, hypocritical set of attitudes is deeply damaging because all honesty is suppressed. 'The code' is the code of social values that holds them all trapped and unable to express individuality in any way.

'A boy in the playground...'

The poem concludes with an elliptical account of the shocking event which broke up the proceedings. The final line of the poem shows how the horror of the moment hangs in the child's memory. 'My mother's mute shame': she has been disgraced so utterly by the child's utterance that her place and standing in her local society are lost for ever. She knows there is nothing she can do to recover it, so she remains mute. 'The taste of soap' recalls the order to 'Wash your mouth out with soap!' which was a common order given to children who had spoken unforgivable words (i.e. expletives).

Recalling this incident many years after it happened, the persona appears to have a complex set of emotions. She may have enjoyed these parties as something out of the humdrum ordinariness of day-to-day life. She was probably quite close to her mother and presumably enjoyed sitting at her feet and listening while appearing to read. But, like all children, she wanted attention, and spoke the forbidden words without fully considering the consequences, but also because she felt compelled to prick the bubble of self-importance and to shock the women out

of their complacency. Did she want to shame her mother and destroy her position in society? No, but with hindsight she is scathingly contemptuous of society's expectations, and feels that it was right to expose its hypocrisy. After all, the women all knew the word; they were not really shocked, but they all pretended to be so in order to preserve their position in a society which demanded such behaviour. All this was long ago, and today such a comment would barely be noticed.

Themes

The themes are nostalgia; the dangers of conformity; implicit criticism of a society that relegated women to such a position; quasi-religious observances replacing conventional religion. Language is also a theme: 'Language embarrassed them', and the persona seems to rub this in by the sophistication of her vocabulary. She shows her contempt in the comment 'certainly not leukaemia, which no one could spell'. Language is the tool she uses in a deliberately unsophisticated way — to break up the intolerant atmosphere.

Style and form

The poem is told as a retrospective account by the persona, many years later, and the language is prepared and fluent. There are a number of striking **similes** and **metaphors**, e.g. 'eyes, hard/as the bright stones in engagement rings'; 'The year a mass grave of wasps bobbed in a jam-jar; a butterfly stammered itself in my curious hands'. These are metaphors of a memorable summer, a time of transition and growing up for the persona; they refer to death (perhaps that of her immature self) and captivity — the butterfly beats its wings in a forlorn attempt to escape from its cage, as the persona does. Compare these with similar references to coming-of-age summers in other poems, e.g. 'That feverish July, the air tasted of electricity' ('In Mrs Tilscher's Class').

At the end of the poem, the grammar breaks down, and mere phrases are enough to evoke what happened. The poem is divided into four stanzas, and the break between the second and third accentuates the phrase 'broken/to bits', which straddles the stanzas.

References and allusions

- 'American Tan', line 5: 'American Tan' was one of the colours nylon tights were available in; they were a relatively rare luxury in the 1960s

'Nostalgia'

Nostalgia is a common theme for Duffy and this can be viewed as her considered thoughts on it: 'a sweet pain in the heart'. It a delicately written poem, with subtle images, observing in the conclusion that even when one returns home it is to find 'everything changed', but **paradoxically** there is 'the same street', the 'same sign on the inn', 'the same bell'. The suggestion is that it is the person returning who has changed rather than the place.

'Stafford Afternoons'

Duffy moved to Stafford from her native Glasgow at the age of 6 and spent the remainder of her childhood there. It is likely that much of her concern with childhood alienation derives from the experience of being uprooted and moved to a culture in which, with her Glasgow accent and urban background, she would have been seen, and no doubt treated, as an outsider.

'Stafford Afternoons', in the plural, suggests that this is how afternoons in Stafford generally were, for the young Duffy at any rate, and no doubt they often started out in this undirected way, a young girl looking for a way to amuse herself. There was, however, presumably only one afternoon which was burned into her memory by meeting the man who exposed himself. The use of the plural perhaps suggests that there was always such a danger lurking behind the familiar, although she had been innocently unaware of it until that day.

The poem is obviously autobiographical, to the extent at least that Duffy spent her childhood afternoons in Stafford, although whether these events actually occurred to her is not clear. The persona is a young girl, perhaps aged between 7 and 11 years, and she tells the story in a retrospective **dramatic monologue** with no indication of any audience. She is innocent and naive, although adventurous too, and sensitive to nature, colours and sounds (was she really so at the time, or is this Duffy colouring the voice of her persona with retrospective subtleties?).

'Only there...': the reader's attention is caught by this arresting opening. Why should it be only there? Is there something unique about Stafford? Or is it unique only in the poet's experience as the place where such traumatic, rite-of-passage events occurred? Note also the distancing effect of making 'the afternoons' the subject of the sentence, as if it was the fault of the afternoons, not of the human actors.

At the beginning of the poem, the persona is in a strange, dreamy, unworldly mood, not securely anchored in her surroundings; the afternoon had 'suddenly pause[d]', and she was alone. She wanders aimlessly, until she comes to the countryside. She is bored, but also lets her imagination run: she 'invented...a vivid lie' for the horse. The boy she passes is 'strange', but she may be transferring her own mood.

Although it can be argued that there is an air of unreality and heightened perceptions from the beginning of the poem ('the afternoon could suddenly pause', 'a long road held no one', 'an ice-cream van chimed and dwindled away'), it becomes significantly more sinister. This occurs in stanza 3, as if the crawling through the hedge has brought her, magically, into another world. She is 'lonely and thrilled', but 'the green silence' 'swallowed' her. Note that from this point on the landscape seems threatening, for example the nettles and the sly shadows of the trees; the man's penis is compared to a root. 'I knew it was dangerous', she says.

These events clearly constituted a traumatic experience for the young girl persona, yet her narration is surprisingly understated, and little reaction is shown or recorded. There are two alternative, and mutually exclusive, possibilities:

(a) She is retelling this soon after the event and before she can fully appreciate its impact (perhaps she is still too traumatised to understand it fully). This could explain the matter-of-fact style, but not the adult-like distance.

(b) Perhaps the story is being told so many years later that its immediacy has faded. This could also explain the matter-of-fact style. After all, the man did not in fact assault or pursue her, although out there in the countryside he could easily have done so, and so although shocking, hindsight shows that the experience could have been much worse — which in no way diminishes its impact at the time, as the final image of the poem dramatically suggests.

The concluding two and a half lines make a terrifying image which sums up the message of the poem: a group of children are innocently playing when an incomprehensible external event shatters their idyll. The agent is described as 'time' because arguably it is the force that is always waiting to snatch away the innocence of children. Time is like a 'red ball' falling from the sky, suddenly and violently — the equivalent of the sun falling on the children. Perhaps this also reminds us that the author of the disaster is an adult, a member of a group until now trusted by the child but now shown to be treacherous, in the same way that the sun is trusted until it falls.

Style and form

This is a composed and grammatical monologue, prepared and delivered as a piece — unlike many of Duffy's monologues. The language is sophisticated and the sentences often complex. The first four stanzas are self-contained and end-stopped. Each begins with a location ('there', 'on the motorway bridge', 'in a cul-de-sac' are the first three; the 'it' of the fourth is just as clearly a reference to place). The transition to the final section (stanzas 5–6) is marked by the only ungrammatical utterance in the poem, the simple, resigned, understated 'Too late'. The mood and grammar change, and the fifth stanza tumbles into the sixth in an echo of the panic in which the girl runs away (it made sound 'rush back', but that is what she did, too).

There are several colour words, and references to colour, in this poem: 'invented, in colour' (line 8); 'the green silence' (line 12); 'light and shade' (line 14); 'silver birch' (line 18); 'purple root' (line 19); 'red ball' (line 24). They add vividness to the picture and emphasise the sensitivity of the girl. The colours become more jarring and out of place (purple, red) after the shock.

Similarly, there are numerous references to sounds or their absence: 'pause' (line 1); 'an ice-cream van chimed' (line 4); sound 'dwindled away' (line 4); 'the noisy field' (line 7); 'the green silence' (line 12); gulping (line 12); wood letting out 'its sticky breath' (line 15); nettles 'gathered spit' (line 16); 'made sound rush back' (line 20); lawnmower (line 20); 'shrieked' (line 23). The sounds are initially normal and harmonious; as the girl goes into her own dream and danger approaches, the normal world is blocked out; after the shock, the sounds of normality return, but there are also abnormal sounds, e.g. the **oxymoron** of the man's 'hoarse, frightful endearments' and the shrieks of the children (as if they, too, were running from the man). The sounds heighten the physical descriptions.

Themes

One theme is innocence and experience: a child's afternoon wanderings through idyllic countryside near her home are scarred by an encounter with the adult world — a man exposes himself and makes improper suggestions to the girl, whose innocence is smashed at a stroke. Another theme could be danger and the unknown hidden among the familiar. The poem has a fairy-tale quality (c.f. Little Red Riding Hood, and Duffy's poem on the subject, 'Little Red-Cap').

'Brothers'

A reflective monologue about the persona's four brothers. She is nostalgic for her childhood, but also looks forward, with resignation, to the day when they will carry her in a box to her grave.

'The Good Teachers'

This is another poem about nostalgia for school days, this time taking as its inspiration the old-style panoramic school photographs in which, because of the slow rate of pan of the camera, it was possible for one child to appear at both ends if he/she ran fast enough. The persona is looking at the photograph, remembering the teachers, those she loved, those she did not, and remembering details, just as in 'Mrs Tilscher's Class'. What follows is a resigned summary of what happened next: growing up, marriage, getting a mortgage ('the Cheltenham and Gloucester' is a building society) and the present. The tone is muted, not regretful but accepting.

'Like Earning a Living'

A display of contempt for the small-minded, unimaginative people who surround the persona. It describes the impoverishment of their thought and language — 'There just aren't the words for it'. The final couplet rearranges a sentence into 'youth speak', and 'He met a poet. Didn't know it' inverts Bob Dylan's original 'I'm a poet. And I know it', adding to the hopeless tone of the poem. It captures the frustration of the intelligent adolescent surrounded by questions that he/she cannot answer and that no one he/she knows would even understand.

'Caul'

A caul is the membrane that covers the head of a baby at birth. It was believed to ward off drowning at sea, so seafarers sought and kept them. The persona thinks

back to the day of her birth, of the selling of the membrane and imagines where it might be now, a part of her: 'I'm all that is left of then.'

'Away and See'

This poem is a meditation about language, but it is also about the need to explore, to move on. 'Away and see' suggests going away and seeing the world. It includes the memorable injunction: 'Test words/wherever they live; listen and touch, smell, believe./Spell them with love.' This is perhaps Duffy's credo as a poet, a passionate statement of her devotion to language.

'Small Female Skull'

In this strange and powerful poem the persona is sitting, alone, holding her head, and imagining that what she holds is her own 'small female skull'. It is as if she is already dead, although the people 'downstairs' suggest she is not. She is reading the story of her life in the skull: 'I see the scar where I fell for pure love'. An ocarina is a small wind instrument.

'Moments of Grace'

This poem links religion, language and love — three of Duffy's major preoccupations. It is also about memory and nostalgia, recalling those moments of grace in everyday life when it seems as if transcendence has been achieved: 'In moments of grace/we were verbs, the secret of poems, talented.'

'The Grammar of Light'

This is a reflective meditation upon the nature of language, light and life. It is grammatically complex, e.g. 'Even barely enough light to find a mouth,/and bless both with a meaningless O, teaches,/spells out'. The repetition of 'the way' creates a litany of images and observations. Light is a religious concept (Christ is the Light of the World). Just as grammar explains and illuminates the ways in which language functions, so the 'Grammar of Light' explains and illuminates the ways in which light operates. The language of the poem is limpid and clear, like the light it describes, e.g. 'The way all faces blur/to dreams of themselves held in the eyes'. It includes many echoes of other poems: the 'wasteground' and 'allotments' remind us of 'Stafford Afternoons', and the waiter balancing light is reminiscent of 'The Other Country'. In the end, the poem is about the transitory and tragic nature of human life, like light: 'The way everything dies.'

'Valentine'

This is not a cynical but an honest view of love: the persona has passed beyond romantic clichés. He/she appears to be at the point of asking whether his/her lover wants their relationship to become marriage — with all that implies — or not. The way the scent of the onion 'clings to your knife' in the end suggests that the poem is about all the stages of love, including heartbreak in the end.

'Close'

This poem is a cryptic meditation upon love. A pair of lovers are in a bedroom, and their 'two childhoods stand in the corner', representing the emotional and historical baggage which each brings to the encounter. This idea is revisited at the end, where 'The ghosts of ourselves/behind and before us, throng in a mirror, blind/laughing and weeping.' How can the lovers enjoy the present in such company?

'Adultery'

Note the relatively unusual use of 'you' by Duffy. The persona reflects upon her adulterous affair, enjoying the excitement, but then considering the consequences: '...illness and debt,/a ring thrown away in a garden/no moon can heal.' She concludes, bitterly, 'and all for the same thing twice' — a line she repeats to reinforce the effect — implying that this love will end up as the previous one has. Then, her grief unravelling her grammar, she admits, in an ambiguous set of juxtapositions in an internal dialogue, that she did do it. The repetition of 'Fuck', first as a descriptive verb, then as an expletive in response, is decoded immediately after, drawing attention, as so often in Duffy's poems, to the ambiguous role of language: 'That was/the wrong verb. This is only an abstract noun.' Their encounters were more emotional than 'fuck' suggests, so it's the wrong word.

'Fraud'

The persona admits immediately to identity theft, but then, more subtly, to a series of manipulations that exploit the corrupt ways of the rich and powerful. His language is as shocking and brutal as the crudity of his moral views. The implication is that many of those in positions of power are just like him: compromised either by money or lustful indiscretion. The poem begins and ends with his name — or names — as if these are all that are, and are not, real. It has been suggested that this poem refers to Robert Maxwell, a media tycoon who was disgraced after his death by the discovery of the extensive frauds he had committed.

'The Biographer'

The male persona is infatuated with the female Victorian poet who is the subject of his biography. A daguerrotype is an early form of photograph. Emma Elizabeth Hibbert is a fictional creation of Duffy's. The empty phrase 'And this is a life' is central and ambiguous: he describes his own life, and the biography he has written is another person's life. The poem is concerned with the derivative nature of the biographer's trade compared with the creativity of its subject; although the persona is sufficiently well regarded to have secured 'a big advance' (i.e. payment before

writing the book), he sees his own face (seen in yet another mirror) as having a 'talentless, dustjacket smile', suggesting that he appreciates how much less distinguished he is than his subject.

'Mean Time'

This is the title poem of the collection, and the title itself embodies multiple ambiguities. The poem is an account of lost love and lost time. It starts with the primitive view that changing the clocks at the end of summer 'steals' time. Time is mean in many senses; the lover is irrevocably gone; but the persona's time is spent turning over in his/her mind 'words I would never have said', full of regret. Light and dark symbolises what time gives, then takes away again.

'Prayer'

A recurring theme in Duffy's poetry is secular replacements for traditional religious observances. 'Litany' is an explicit example; this is another. Prayers represent the ritual and repetition of daily life: the clattering of a train's wheels over the joints in the track mimicking Latin declensions once said aloud; the chorus of mothers calling their children at dusk (see also 'Moments of Grace'); the litany of the shipping forecast on Radio 4, a comforting catalogue of exotically named, dangerous places. The familiar repetition brings a sense of reassurance that the world is fundamentally unchanging, like a prayer does. Note that, unusually, this poem **rhymes**, like a prayer.

The World's Wife

Background

Following the success of her first four collections of poems, all of which cover broadly similar ground, Duffy published *The World's Wife* in 1999. It is her first themed collection, and is more consistently and overtly feminist than much of her earlier work. Other themes also achieve a much greater prominence, namely religion and classical mythology, as well as a number of explicit language games. In the process, though, a central feature of Duffy's earlier work is lost: because the title of every poem names the wife or female counterpart of a historical or mythological figure, the challenge for the reader of identifying the narrating persona is removed. This leads to a certain uniformity, despite Duffy's efforts to achieve variety, and reduces the scope for the kind of ironic ambiguities that abound in the earlier collections. The majority of the poems are told as retrospective narratives, often with a considerable period of time having elapsed since the events they relate, giving a sense of distance rare in Duffy's earlier poems. All are, of course, about women.

Female voices

The tone of *The World's Wife* is more relentless and unapologetically feminist than Duffy's previous collections. A large number of the personas it includes are witheringly contemptuous of the men they have ended up with, who are generally inadequate, self-obsessed and immature. More generally, men are depicted as useless, incompetent, arrogant, vain and, ultimately, unnecessary. Women are resourceful, sturdy and above all capable of taking on the roles traditionally ascribed by society to men. This is an important corrective, especially in the historical contexts in which many of the poems are set. Some poems plausibly represent the likely viewpoint of these unrecorded women; others are counter-factual, such as 'The Kray Sisters', which is an alternative version of history of the 'What if…' school, an increasingly popular **genre** in the 1990s and into the 2000s.

The title of the collection is itself a clever overturning of the well-known phrase, 'the world and his wife'; this deeply patronising utterance implies that, in all places and at all times, only men are of importance, and their wives are mere appendages. Duffy gives a voice to these previously unheard women, both as individuals and — as 'the world's wife' — as archetypes of how women respond to male domination and male annexation of credit for ideas and acts that may not have been truly theirs.

Myth and history

An important difference from the earlier collections is the proportion of poems in *The World's Wife* set either in a historical past before Duffy's own experience, or in biblical and mythological times. In this she focuses on what has been a central concern of women writers in the postmodernist movement, which started in the 1960s: the role of mythology in establishing the dominance of men and submission of women. No fewer than 11 of the 30 poems in the collection involve characters from Greek mythology, some transported into a contemporary setting as archetypes, the majority left in their original time. Similarly, there is a higher proportion of poems than in previous collections that deal with Christian themes or characters, although their overall tone is more explicitly atheistic than in Duffy's earlier work.

Historical translations

A number of the poems take historical or mythological characters and translate them to the present day, with the striking result that they are belittled by the trivial, middle-class existences they are forced to lead. 'Mrs Midas' turns the noble king of Phrygia into a pathetic, avaricious, middle-aged man, and 'Mrs Tiresias' sees Tiresias, having become female, experiencing the frustrations and pleasures of being a modern woman.

There is, however, an element of 'double-think' (Orwell's term in *Nineteen Eighty-Four* for holding two incompatible opinions simultaneously) in the portrayal of these transferred characters. What is the relationship between the modern Midas

and the eighth-century BC king? The poem is a fantasy anyway, because a 'golden touch' does not literally exist. Is it a metaphor? If so, it is not really pursued; Midas is a rather pathetic character who does not seem particularly greedy. He appears to become more like his mythological forebear, but it is not clear what the implications of this are. Similarly, Mrs Aesop speaks as if the phrases and fables repeated by her husband are familiar, over-used and stale — which could hardly have been the case when the original Aesop wrote them. It is difficult to reconcile the alternatives logically, leaving the reader in a tantalising, half-factual, half-fictional world that cannot be properly tied down — exciting interest but also frustration.

Fortunately there are exceptions to the prevailing pattern of abused and neglected wives. In 'Anne Hathaway', Shakespeare's wife proves herself to be a poet just as gifted as her husband (is the implication, comparable to that of 'Mrs Darwin', that she actually wrote his works?), and the resulting **sonnet** is a delightful mixture of affection, poetic references and linguistic playfulness. 'The Kray Sisters' presents a feminist alternative history in Cockney rhyming slang; 'Demeter', the concluding poem, brings us a lyrical vision of how the birth of a daughter can transcend time and culture.

Reversals

A key and recurring feature of these poems is the reversal of expectations and assumptions. Queen Kong is a remarkably tender giant gorilla, falling in love with a human; Mrs Beast is perhaps the most brazen assertion of an alternative, macho-feminist view of women— man may be the Beast, but woman is at least his equal; Mrs Faust neatly turns the Faust legend: 'I keep Faust's secret still —/the clever, cunning, callous bastard/didn't have a soul to sell'; Penelope is 'most certainly not waiting' for Odysseus to return.

The poems that deal with Bible stories are among the most interesting of the reversal poems, if only because in her earlier poems Duffy suggested at least an aesthetic sympathy for the Catholicism in which she was brought up. Queen Herod is warned by 'Three Queens' of the birth of a not-at-all Christ-like figure — '*Adulterer. Bigamist./The Wolf*' — and resolves to have him slaughtered to defend her new-born baby daughter from his advances. In 'Pilate's Wife' Pilate's wife comments: 'Was he God? Of course not. Pilate believed he was.'

Poet and persona

The personas (the voices in which Duffy writes) of *The World's Wife* are certainly expressing the inner and unspoken secrets of their characters. Duffy acts as a channel between their silent thoughts and the audience, which is compelled to share the persona's perspective. The old uncertainty about where the persona's voice ends and Duffy's begins has now become irrelevant, as they are all her creations, and we can therefore say with greater confidence that the voices of the personas correspond with Duffy's own views — which no doubt explains the clear, some might say jarring, tones in which themes such as feminism, often understated in her earlier poetry, have now become prominent.

'Little Red-Cap'

In this feminist reversal of the Little Red Riding Hood legend, the girl seizes the initiative for her own purposes. The poem is also about innocence and experience: the persona deliberately goes into the woods with the intention of losing her innocence on her own terms. It contains the fine image 'allotments/kept, like mistresses, by kneeling married men', which presages the way in which the persona is kept by 'the wolf'.

'Thetis'

Thetis was one of the nereids (see 'Circe'). She was fated to bear a son mightier than its father, hence the ending of the poem. The legend is taken out of its Greek setting and becomes the metaphorical voyage of a shape-changing woman as she tries to elude the man who seeks her as his wife.

'Queen Herod'

This is a dramatic monologue. Queen Herod is visited by three female Magi who bring gifts for her new-born daughter, and also prophesy that a star will announce the birth of the daughter's consort. Queen Herod is horrified and dispatches soldiers to kill all the male babies. This is an alternative, feminist explanation for the traditional reason for the slaughter of the innocents at the time of the birth of Christ. 'We wade through blood/for our sleeping girls', she memorably says, an image of the timeless duty of mothers to protect their daughters.

'Mrs Midas'

The legend of King Midas has several components. He was King of Phrygia, perhaps in the eighth century BC. He is famous for being granted 'the golden touch' — everything he touched literally turned to gold (the phrase is now used metaphorically). He is also famous for having 'ass's ears', a punishment for poor judgement. Although Duffy makes no reference to this part of the myth she probably assumes that readers would be familiar with it.

This is one of a number of poems in the collection in which a well-known historical or mythological personage is transplanted into a modern context. The effect in this case is trivialisation. For a king in classical Greece to be surrounded by gold was expected; in a suburban semi, it is utterly incongruous. This Midas is not noble in any sense; he is pathetic, and can be dismissed as 'the fool/who wished for gold'. Note that the phrase 'Midas touch' is commonly used to denote someone with a gift for making money, and in one sense the poem can be seen as another example of Duffy actualising a metaphor, in this case the 'golden touch'. The setting

is clearly contemporary: a caravan and driving are mentioned in stanza 9. Mr and Mrs Midas live in a comfortable suburban house with a long garden, and their taste for dry Italian wine suggests they are typically middle class. Presumably Duffy wishes to bring the Midas story into a more familiar environment, and to ask what effect such a transformation might have upon present-day people.

The problem, of course, is that Midas has not thought through the consequences of his wish: turning everything he touches to gold makes eating, for example, impossible. Mrs Midas is initially frightened, both for herself and for the cat, which she locks in the cellar. Midas presumably never touches her again.

Very little impression is formed of the character of Mr Midas. He has no voice and does not seem to do anything apart from react to his situation and accept the decisions made by his wife. He may therefore be weak. His wife refers to him as a 'fool' and accuses him of 'idiocy', 'greed', 'lack of thought' and 'selfishness'. The reference in the penultimate stanza to him 'hearing the music of Pan' may mean that he is going mad, or that he is adapting to his new situation.

Indeed, the entire story is related through the eyes of Mrs Midas (the persona). The husband's voice is virtually never heard in *The World's Wife*, and it is always an open question as to whether the impression given by a bitter wife is the whole truth. Mrs Midas is curiously detached from the extraordinary events she has witnessed, e.g. 'I served up the meal'. She is dismissive of her husband, but shows no interest in how he acquired his golden touch. Perhaps they inhabit a world where such things are common, in which case it is not our world (a common difficulty with the poems in *The World's Wife* that have been transferred from their original context). It is as if the circumstances of this miracle are of no interest to Mrs Midas at all; she has to live with the consequences. Midas seems feeble, weak, unable to establish his presence, and accedes to the arrangements she puts in place for him without protest, including his exile to the caravan. Perhaps he was always feeble-minded; perhaps, as stanza 10 suggests, he was not fully in touch with normal reality.

There is a suggestion in the penultimate stanza that the contemporary Midas may be becoming assimilated with his classical namesake. Pan was the Greek god of the woods and of music; the reference may imply that Midas is becoming more attuned to the classical roots of his condition, or is fusing with the mythological original. Perhaps more importantly, this may be an oblique reference to the next lot of trouble King Midas got himself into after the golden touch, when he was chosen as the judge for the musical contest between Apollo and Pan. When Midas chose Pan, Apollo was offended and turned Midas's ears into those of an ass. When in the poem Mr Midas hears Pan's music issuing from the woods, perhaps it will all be a little bit of history repeating?

Mrs Midas narrates all this from the perspective of something that happened long ago and on which she can now look back and reflect. By the end of the poem she is mostly reconciled to what has happened. Perhaps to her own surprise she finds that she does sometimes miss Midas's physical presence. The style of the language (its register, complexity and subtlety of diction) is always the key to emotion, tone and mood. Perhaps the closing mood is one of regret rather than anger.

Language and style

The mood changes as the poem proceeds, reaching a crescendo of fear in the middle part before settling back to a tone of resignation. The language at the beginning of the poem is smooth, sophisticated and flows in long, well-crafted grammatical sentences. There are elaborate metaphors, depicting Mrs Midas as educated, fluent and sensitive, e.g. 'steamy breath/gently blanching the windows'. At the crisis the diction abruptly changes: the sentences become short, staccato and functional, employing a simple, factual vocabulary ('I locked the cat in the cellar. I moved the phone'). The effect is to make the actions seem immediate and urgent, almost panicky, and to speed the narration, which had been languorous at the start. Once the crisis is over, she reverts to her earlier, more relaxed and more elevated style: 'its amber eyes/holding their pupils like flies.'

The language of this poem is in an elevated register and there are a number of instances of unusual vocabulary, striking diction and clever poetic effect. Here are some examples:

- 'The kitchen…blanching the windows': the metaphor suggests that the whole kitchen is cooking
- 'wiped the other's glass like a brow': the simile reinforces the impression that, unwittingly, Mrs Midas and the kitchen are sweating as if there is tension in the air
- 'Now the garden was long and the visibility poor': the 'now' gives distance and perspective to the observation and is an indication that these events happened some time ago; it is also a way of excusing the observer for not immediately noticing the transformation
- 'You know the mind': i.e. you know how the mind works
- 'like a king on a burnished throne': in the original myth Midas is a king and gold is associated with royalty
- 'glass, goblet, golden chalice': the words alliteratively echo the physical trans-formation of the glass, but also reflect the increasing status of the vessel as it becomes more suited to a king
- 'Look, we all have wishes; granted./But who has wishes granted? Him': Duffy uses clever wordplay, in which 'granted', an indication of assent to the preceding truism, is then echoed as part of a rhetorical question, which is then in turn subverted by answering 'Him'. This is a good example of Duffy's intelligent verbal humour.

- 'aurum' and 'luteous' indicate a highly sophisticated vocabulary: 'aurum' is Latin for gold; 'luteous' means golden-yellow, and is derived from Latin. The classical origins of these words match the origins of the Midas story.
- 'a heart of gold': another subverted cliché; it usually refers to people who are caring, but a literal 'heart of gold' leads to another cliché — Midas literally becomes 'hard-hearted'
- 'his child…ore limbs…amber eyes…': a delicately beautiful set of images to evoke the imaginary gold-child
- 'I woke to the streaming sun': note that the colour and light words and images convey goldenness

Themes

The themes are greed; foolishness; failure to consider the consequences of actions. These are failings typical of the men in Duffy's world (see also 'Mrs Aesop').

References and allusions

- 'blanching', line 4: to plunge meat, green vegetables etc. into boiling water or bring to the boil in water in order to whiten, preserve the natural colour, or reduce or remove a bitter or salty taste; the windows are whitened by the steam
- 'Fondante d'Automne', line 10: a variety of pear
- 'Field of the Cloth of Gold', line 15: a celebrated encounter between the kings of England and France in 1520; both attempted to outdo the other by the magnificence of their entourages, which made the whole field seem golden
- 'Miss Macready', line 15: presumably Mrs Midas's history teacher at school
- 'the tomb of Tutankhamun', line 39: the tomb of an Egyptian pharoah, splendidly gilded; there was a celebrated exhibition in London in the 1960s of the treasures found there — the spare room will also be full of treasures
- 'burnished throne', line 16: 'burnished' means shiny, smooth or polished; a reference to Shakespeare's *Antony and Cleopatra* (II.2.191)
- 'Halcyon days', line 40: this is now taken to mean a time of peace or happiness; originally, in Greek mythology, it referred to the 14 days in midwinter when the kingfisher laid its eggs and the weather was perfectly still

'*from* Mrs Tiresias'

Tiresias is a character from Ancient Greek mythology who was turned into a woman for 7 years after he hit two copulating serpents with a stick; he was subsequently better known as a blind seer. Duffy adapts this myth for her own purposes, moving Tiresias into a contemporary setting and having him irrevocably change gender to become a woman. The poem then becomes, in part, a vehicle for feminist comments about the inability of men to cope with being a woman ('Then he started his period. One week in bed./Two doctors in./Three painkillers four times a day'). After he leaves, Mrs Tiresias begins a lesbian relationship, and the poem ends memorably with her new lover meeting her ex-husband: 'the clash of their sparkling rings and their painted nails'.

'Pilate's Wife'

This is a characteristic rewriting of a Bible story. Pilate's wife, bored with her lot, finds Christ ('the Nazarene') sexually attractive, but is unable to persuade Pilate to spare him: 'Was he God? Of course not. Pilate believed he was.'

'Mrs Aesop'

Aesop lived on the Greek island of Samos in the sixth century BC. He wrote a collection of more than 650 fables — short tales, often with animal characters, that illustrate a moral. They have been translated and retold many times and are a fundamental part of Western culture. Most of the poem consists of turning, misquoting or subverting Aesop's fables and other well-known proverbs and sayings.

This is an angry poem, as the rather shocking opening suggests. It also clearly establishes the setting as **anachronistic**, as Aesop's life predated that of Christ by 600 years. Aesop and his wife have been transferred from their historical context of Ancient Greece. It is hard to specifically identify where they have been planted — the idiom is modern, but that is typical of Duffy, and there is no explicit evidence of a contemporary setting. This ambiguity is appropriate for fables, which are meant to be timelessly relevant.

The tense of the narrative is interesting. The use of completed past tenses perhaps suggests that the events are a long time in the past and that Aesop is now dead. If so, it is surprising that Mrs Aesop remains so bitter; her final comment, also quoting a familiar adage, gives the impression that her pleasure in her victory remains strong.

The impression the reader forms of Mrs Aesop (the persona) is not necessarily favourable. Aesop may be annoying, but there is no evidence that he mistreated her to any significant degree. The intemperate and blasphemous opening of the poem perhaps suggests that she is irascible and intolerant. Her attitude is maintained unrelentingly until the bitter end: 'I laughed last, longest.'

Aesop is presented as a boring, tedious pedant, who sees everything through the ideas and images of his fables, and is despised for it by his wife. Mrs Aesop is utterly contemptuous of her husband, but as there is no evidence of his point of view the reader cannot form a fair judgement. Mrs Aesop is clearly not reconciled to her fate: she is one of the most unrelentingly bitter of *The World's Wife* characters, although she has not suffered as much as others, so the reader may be somewhat unsympathetic towards her. However, her withering contempt for Aesop is somewhat tempered by the humour with which she delivers it.

There is a typical Duffy doublethink conceit here: she gives the impression that all these tales and proverbs are dull because they are so familiar, but to the original

Aesop they could not possibly have been. Duffy's Mrs Aesop seems like a twentieth-century version, and perhaps she is: perhaps, like Mrs Midas, this is merely a namesake, centuries later, which would justify the contempt because, unlike the original Aesop, he did not conceive of these fables; he merely repeats them *ad nauseam*. Perhaps Duffy deliberately conflates the original Aesop and a modern version to subvert reader expectation.

Style and language

The language is unsophisticated and is often ungrammatical, but much of it is based upon quotation from, or is a direct parody of, fables; the writing is clever and witty.

The stanzas are all end-stopped except for the penultimate one, in which Duffy uses her characteristic enjambement to create an ambiguity, e.g. 'And that's another thing, the sex', but in full this reads 'the sex/was diabolical'. There are a number of internal rhymes (e.g. prepossess/impress, shy/sly/sky) and instances of alliteration (e.g. 'I laughed last, longest').

Themes

The theme is that a lack of imagination and originality leads to an impoverished linguistic diet of clichés and platitudes.

References and allusions

- 'Purgatory', line 1: in Roman Catholicism, a place where the dead go to be purged of their sins before being allowed to enter heaven; they undergo punishment if their sins merit it. For non-Catholics, purgatory is a place of suffering or torment, especially one that is temporary.

'Mrs Darwin'

A brilliant and dismissive **epigram**: is Mrs Darwin suggesting that she had the idea of the theory of evolution, or is she just confirming the theory by pointing out how ape-like her husband is?

'Mrs Sisyphus'

Sisyphus was an Ancient Greek condemned to roll a boulder up a hill for eternity; it rolled back down immediately. He is therefore a symbol for pointless activity. The poem is partly a language game (note the number of rhymes and **half-rhymes**, which give a sense of repetition that imitates Sisyphus's punishment) but also shows us another wife despairing of the obsessive behaviour of her husband.

'Mrs Faust'

This poem is written in a casual, throwaway contemporary style which suits its setting. Mrs Faust does just as well as her husband out of the bargain, but Duffy then subverts the myth at the end: 'I keep Faust's secret still —/the clever, cunning, callous bastard/didn't have a soul to sell.' By implication the poem subverts Christianity as well, because if Faust has no soul then he wins from the bargain: the point of the original story was that he realised, at the end, that he had made a disastrous choice.

'Delilah'

This poem is based on a story from the Bible. Samson was famously strong, but his strength resided in his hair, which Delilah cut off (thereby making her a proto-feminist icon, one of the first to fight back). The setting is anachronistic; this is one of several poems in the collection that embody the paradox that they are both historical and metaphorical at the same time, in that this both *is* the biblical couple, (so that Samson's loss of hair *does* deprive him of his strength) and also a modern metaphorical couple in which the woman seizes the power in the relationship.

'Anne Hathaway'

Anne Hathaway was Shakespeare's wife, but her maiden name is used to mark the unusual fact that she was known as Anne Hathaway rather than as Mrs Shakespeare. It is based on the curious clause in Shakespeare's will quoted as the epigraph, and is written in the form of a Shakespearian sonnet. It is a tender meditation upon poetry and love. Like 'Queen Kong', Anne Hathaway is one of the independent female characters in the collection who are not abused by their male partner.

'Queen Kong'

King Kong was a giant gorilla who terrorised the citizens of New York in a celebrated horror film of 1933. There was no Queen Kong — Duffy has invented her as his female counterpart. Queen Kong is not King Kong's wife; this is one of the poems in which Duffy subverts her own model for the collection, which could more accurately be called *The World's Wife, or Feminist Counterparts of Famous Males*. If there had been a similar female giant gorilla, how would she have behaved? Not by terrorising the inhabitants of New York, it seems, but by tenderly and romantically falling for a tiny human. The plot parallels that of the original film quite closely in moving from the tropical island to New York.

There is, however, a huge and insuperable paradox at the heart of the poem, which is fundamentally mischievous. Queen Kong is, much of the time, a giant gorilla on the scale of the original King Kong: 'I could swat his plane from these skies like a gnat', she says. But, completely unaccountably, she is also able to go shopping in Bloomingdale's. (How could she get through the door? Are the staff accustomed to serving gorillas, regardless of their size? How did she acquire the dollars? How many gorilla clothes does Bloomingdale's stock?) Once this is noticed, it becomes clear that the poem cannot in any sense be taken 'literally'.

This poem is a clear example of Duffy reversing the reader's expectations. King Kong terrorised American film audiences with his size, his power and his temper. Queen Kong might therefore be expected to be equally destructive, and for Duffy to make her gentle and sentimental is surprising for the reader. Perhaps she wanted to undermine the prejudice that gorillas are violent and insensitive, or more generally to call into question unreflective judgements about the unfamiliar. There is also, of course, a reversal of the 'beauty and the beast' myth upon which the original film is based: King Kong, the beast, terrorises the helpless beauty, played by Fay Wray; a female beast, by contrast, is gentle to the male beauty she carries off.

Equally, the human became fond of Queen Kong (by her account) and appears to have been happy to go to the island where he would 'sit, cross-legged, near my ear/for hours'. Queen Kong is loyal and affectionate, and is clearly very fond of her 'little man'. She pursued him to New York, brought him back to her island and loved him for 12 years before his death. She is **anthropomorphised**, emotionally at least.

There are some clever and unexpected ideas and images which illustrate the reversal of expectations and roles. For example, in stanza 2 she scoops up the 'little man' in a direct parallel to the famous scene in King Kong in which Fay Wray is scooped up — but not quite so tenderly. Stanza 3 suggests a surprisingly erotic element: 'There were things he could do/for me with the sweet finesse of those hands/that no gorilla could.' The affection of the man for Queen Kong also leads to unexpected images: 'He slept in my fur, woke early/to massage the heavy lids of my eyes'; the final image is of the man being carried, as a totem, around Queen Kong's neck: 'No man/has been loved more.'

Language and style

The tone of the poem is surprisingly tender. The story is told as a retrospective monologue by Queen Kong, and the whole tone is of gentle, satisfied resignation: this was the (requited) love of her life, and it came to its natural end. The language is grammatical, relatively formal, precise and clear, reflecting contentment: 'I wear him now about my neck,/perfect, preserved, with tiny emeralds for eyes.'

Themes

The themes could be: not to give way to prejudice or preconceptions; to consider the feelings and humanity of animals; that expectations can be subverted. Duffy goes to some lengths to humanise Queen Kong in order to encourage the reader to reconsider prejudices about gorillas. This is another example of Duffy's use of film as a source for her poems. It is also one of several in *The World's Wife* in which the female plays the dominant role in the relationship.

References and allusions

- 'the Village', line 5: Greenwich Village, one of the most fashionable and intellectual areas of New York
- 'pastrami on rye', line 7: a typical New York delicacy — slices of spiced beef on rye bread
- 'trews', line 27: traditional Scottish tartan trousers; in this context the use is probably patronising
- 'the Hudson', line 43: New York is situated on the mouth of the Hudson River
- 'Bloomingdale's', line 56: a fashionable New York department store
- 'Empire State Building', line 61: the world's tallest building from its construction in 1931 until the World Trade Center was built in 1970; it featured prominently in *King Kong*
- 'Brooklyn Bridge', line 62: a famous bridge in New York

'Mrs Quasimodo'

Quasimodo was the ugly bell ringer and hunchback in *Notre Dame de Paris*, a novel by Victor Hugo. Quasimodo soon tires of his wife, and the poem is a feminist comment on men's obsession with women's outward appearance and the pressure this places upon women. Mrs Quasimodo takes revenge by cutting the clappers out of his bells (a highly sexual image suggestive of castration), culminating with the memorable image of 'the murdered music of the bells'.

'Medusa'

In Greek myth Medusa was one of the Gorgons. Her gaze could turn any living thing to stone and she had snakes instead of hair. She is therefore another proto-feminist with the power to fight back against men. But Duffy adapts this to draw parallels between Medusa's terrifying appearance and the ageing process. She turns her wrath on her cheating husband who surrounds himself with 'your girls, your girls'. The mythological Medusa was slain by Perseus, who used his shield as a mirror to kill her without looking at her directly. Here, Medusa's husband, coming at the end with his shield and sword, may be assumed to be intent on killing her.

'The Devil's Wife'

The poem is a contemporary metaphor: this is a Devil who can seduce a woman in everyday life — literally, in this case, with sexual passion — and lead her to perdition. Neither Christianity nor Greek mythology provide a release from the literal and metaphorical prison to which the Devil has led her. The poem is, unusually, divided into five numbered sections that reflect the stages of the persona's life and condemnation. On Radio 4's *Book Club*, Duffy stated that 'The Devil's Wife' was based on Myra Hindley.

'Circe'

This is one of many poems in *The World's Wife* based upon characters from Greek mythology. Circe is a character in Homer's great mythological poem *The Odyssey*, which tells the epic story of the homecoming of Odysseus to Ithaca after the Trojan War (the poem 'Penelope' refers to another part of the same story). Odysseus has to overcome many obstacles and temptations on his long journey, including Circe, a witch who turned his comrades into pigs. After Odysseus had liberated them, he slept with Circe and remained with her for a year.

'Men are pigs'

The whole poem is an extended and rather vicious feminist metaphor, an elaborate revenge fantasy based on a literalisation of the feminist claim that men are pigs. It is possible to see Circe as an early manifestation of a woman taking revenge on men.

Circe is unusual in this collection in that her existence and importance do not depend upon a man. However, the Circe of the poem is at first sight very different from the character in *The Odyssey*. The principal similarity is that both Circes are surrounded by men who have become pigs. Whereas the Homeric Circe was responsible for the transformation of her victims, in the poem the metaphor is so sustained that it is hard to believe that these pigs were ever men, although the reader assumes that that was the case — or at least, that they represent human men.

Any sensitive reader, especially one familiar with the phrase 'male chauvinist pig', is likely to quickly suspect that these pigs are really men Circe has known. The 'skills of the tongue' in stanza 2 seem very human, and the description of the faces more so; but the real giveaway comes in the third stanza when she says 'did it listen, ever, to you', not in the context of the pig-farmer but as a lover. Once the reader appreciates the metaphor, the treatment of the pigs becomes ever more clearly a matter not of cookery but of sweetly-savoured revenge for the injustices and abuse suffered by Circe (and all women, for whom she stands) at the hands of men. Circe admits at the end of the poem that when she was younger she was 'hoping for men'. But she makes it quite clear that with age and wisdom she no longer does so.

In the third stanza, Circe's vicious dismembering of the pig–man reaches its height. She lingers on the lashing open of the sexual equipment, and moves on to the heart (which is hard, like that of a man), and insists 'dice it small', i.e. destroy it utterly. The repetition links the two stanzas: it marks both the end of the frenzy of hatred, and the introduction to the more philosophical fourth stanza where she remembers an earlier, more romantic time when she was still interested in men. The phrase should be spoken more softly and reflectively the second time to mark the change of mood.

Setting

The setting of the poem is deliberately ambiguous, because although it appears to be in the same period as *The Odyssey*, the public cookery lesson seems rather a modern concept. The poem is perhaps a parody of the genre of television cookery programmes. The tall ships, however, seem to be from the Homeric age. The ambiguity makes the poem timeless.

The poem is unusual in being directly addressed to an audience. The style is of a television cookery programme, and although the audience (of young female spirits) is addressed it makes no contribution or response, strengthening the impression that they may not really be there (as in a television show). Alternatively, she may be surrounded by an attentive circle of young admirers watching her demonstrate how to deal with pigs/men. The form of address, 'nereids and nymphs', is patronising and stereotyped (like 'boys and girls'), has the effect of showing Circe's authority, and also reinforces the Homeric setting, as well as a sense of unreality — these are, after all, spirits, not people. Nevertheless, the ostensible audience confirms that this is a public speech, and the polished and fluent language also supports this view. 'I want to begin with…' continues the television-show style.

Language and tone

The poem's diction is complex and lyrical at times: 'the moon/like a lemon popped in the mouth of the sky'; 'three black ships sighed in the shallow waves'. Elsewhere it includes slang, e.g. 'yobby, porky colognes'. The lyrical language is used of Circe and her feelings; the colloquial language is used of the pigs.

There are some clever, characteristic, and in places shocking uses of language by Duffy in this poem. Here are some striking examples:

- 'a recipe from abroad/which uses the cheek — and the tongue in cheek/at that': a clever actualisation of a metaphor, a common Duffy device
- 'to lie/in the soft pouch of a face': double meaning is achieved by placing 'to lie' at the end of the line; the tongue rests inside the cheeks, but also tells lies
- 'Well-cleaned pig's ears': another actualised metaphor; a 'pig's ear' is a phrase for the kind of mess that presumably men make of things, and here they are also literal ears
- 'the sweetmeats slipped/from the slit, bulging, vulnerable bag of the balls': the list of adjectives emphasises the pleasure that Circe clearly derives from emasculating her victims

Themes

The poem is an elaborate revenge fantasy based on the extended metaphor of men being pigs. It is a feminist poem because of Circe's unrelenting hatred of men, who are portrayed as being devoid of any saving graces. The final stanza shows that Circe did not always view men in this way but has been disillusioned. The poem embodies the themes of the treacherous nature of men; their pig-like appetites; their lies; the pleasure of revenge. It can also be seen as another poem inviting us to look at cuisine from the animal's point of view (see 'A Healthy Meal'); male readers, in particular, may feel uncomfortable when reading Circe's treatment of the pigs.

- 'nereids and nymphs', line 1: nereids are female sea spirits; nymphs are female nature spirits

'Mrs Lazarus'

In this haunting reworking of the Lazarus story, Mrs Lazarus grieves for her bereavement in a historical context, which appears to be later than the Bible but probably not contemporary. The moment when the mood changes is marked by the repetition of 'I knew' in stanza 7. But it is not a joyful reunion, nor is the resurrected Lazarus returning in triumph: it is a vision of horror. It is a retrospective, rather dismissive account, like many others in *The World's Wife*.

'Pygmalion's Bride'

Pygmalion was an ancient Greek sculptor who created a statue so beautiful that he wished for it to come to life. The goddess Aphrodite granted his wish; the statue became Galatea and they were happy together. However, the poem, which is told from the perspective of the statue, presents events very differently. Duffy has turned the story into a timeless archetype of man–woman relations based on the premise that all men want from a relationship is sex. The statue is initially cold and metaphorically like stone; she resists his advances but he still persisits. She then changes tactics by giving in and responding. After they have slept together he, as she knew he would, leaves.

'Mrs Rip Van Winkle'

This is the familiar story of Rip van Winkle, the character in a fairy story by Washington Irving who fell asleep for 20 years, but in Duffy's hands his sleep becomes his wife's liberation: she has the opportunity to do all the things she couldn't do as a wife. Like Mrs Lazarus, she is not pleased when he awakes and expects everything to be the same as before.

'Mrs Icarus'

Another brilliantly **epigrammatic** poem that sums up many women's experience of men. The Icarus myth is transferred to the present day; presumably he is attempting to fly a hang-glider. In the original myth, Icarus flew effortlessly and did not need repeated failed attempts from a 'hillock'.

'Frau Freud'

This monologue, written in a style and with a tone similar to 'Circe', is delivered to a group of women; after showing off her knowledge of slang expressions for the penis — the ludicrous terms exposing it to ridicule — Frau Freud dismisses the object in question with withering contempt. 'Ms M. Lewinsky' is Monica Lewinsky, who famously had oral sex with President Bill Clinton of the USA in the 1990s. 'Penis envy' was one of Freud's most celebrated (and controversial) theories.

'Salome'

Salome was a biblical dancer who asked for, and was given, the head of John the Baptist on a platter. Duffy's Salome is a contemporary version, where her indifference to the identity of the head on the pillow beside her is a cruel reversal of expectation: her indifference, not even remembering his name, reduces the significance of the original to the everyday. Note the colloquial and inappropriate language register, which reinforces the lack of feeling, and the repetition of '-tter' words. The poem opens with a brilliantly subverted metaphor: 'I'd done it before [...] woke up with a head on the pillow beside me'. But in this case it is a severed head.

'Eurydice'

In Greek mythology Eurydice was the wife of Orpheus. After her death from a snake bite, Orpheus sought to rescue Eurydice from the underworld. Hades and Persephone, king and queen of the underworld, allowed Orpheus to bring Eurydice back with him, on the condition that he did not look back at her until they reached the mortal realm. Duffy's Eurydice, in a predictable reversal, is perfectly happy in the underworld until Orpheus comes for her. By calling him 'Big O' she again belittles the original stature of Orpheus, and transfers him to the contemporary world of typewriters and publishers (a telling aside: 'the Gods are like publishers,/usually male'). She does her utmost to thwart his goal by making him look back, and finally succeeds, ironically, by flattering him. This is a monologue, but again addressed to an audience of 'girls' — presumably all those others lucky enough to have escaped their men by dying. The underworld is 'a place where language stopped', presumably because death is the end of all creation and creativity. The poem ends with the moving lines: 'The living walk by the edge of a vast lake/near the wise, drowned silence of the dead.' This might allude to the debt all living writers owe to the achievements of their dead predecessors.

'The Kray Sisters'

Ronnie and Reggie Kray, the Kray twins, were a notorious pair of criminal gangsters from London's East End in the 1960s. Although they ran a protection racket and arranged murders, the pair were viewed with a sentimental fondness by the East End working class, and became folk heroes. Duffy imagines what it would have been like if the Kray twins had been women rather than men.

These sisters are more than female equivalents to the Kray twins because of the explicitly feminist aspects of their 'reign' in London. Despite the personas' attempts to seem threatening, they do not actually seem criminal. They take pride principally in the creation of their feminist night-clubs, with the archetypal names 'Ballbreakers'

and 'Prickteasers', and their highest achievement is persuading Nancy Sinatra to sing her feminist anthem in their club. Although it is not explicitly stated that anyone has been murdered or even beaten up, the sisters are not soft, and there are a number of hints at the threat of violence at least, e.g. 'a threatening word', the double meaning of 'clout' (authority but also a physical blow), and the fact that they 'leaned on Sinatra'. There is a suggestion of violence and menace behind the chirpy tone, which is masked by sentimentality, as for the real Krays. It is another over-turning of a stereotype for Duffy to present women as being as capable of violence as men.

Here are some examples to illustrate this theme of the reversal of readers' expectations:

- 'A boyfriend's for Christmas, not just for life': a parody and reversal of the National Canine Defence League's 1990s slogan 'a dog is for life, not just for Christmas'
- 'Protection': instead of the criminal 'protection racket' operated by the Kray twins, the Kray sisters offered literal protection to any woman who was being abused by a man, although the capitalisation of 'Protection' and 'no questions asked' are echoes of a more criminal activity
- 'we'd leaned on Sinatra to sing for free': the obvious expectation is that they mean Frank, a misapprehension that lingers for six lines until 'her throat' reveals they are referring to Nancy

Style and language

The style is conversational and idiomatic; it is a convincing representation of cockney rhyming slang. Duffy is careful to make it possible for a reader to work out the rhyming slang with a little imagination, and she uses various other colloquialisms to sustain the impression that this is street-talk, e.g. 'straight up', 'clout', 'dosh'.

The mood of the poem is confident, chirpy and almost defiant, as if the persona is daring someone to deny the achievement of the sisters, e.g. 'swaggering into our club'. This reflects both the stereotype of an East Ender and the impression generally held of the real Kray twins. 'Leave us both there' (line 68) suggests that this monologue is looking back, rather wistfully, to the sisters' glory days. The real Kray twins were sentenced to life imprisonment, but there is no reason why the non-criminal Kray sisters should be spending their lives behind bars; perhaps they are merely reminiscing, many years on.

Themes

The poem has the feminist message that women, given a chance, can do as well as men can, even in such a traditionally male-dominated field as being a gangster and running a protection racket. It suggests the distinctive character and social cohesion of the East End and is another example of Duffy looking back to the 1960s.

References and allusions

Much of the poem is written in cockney rhyming slang.

- 'geezers', line 1: men
- 'frog and toad', line 2: road
- 'Savile Row', line 3: the road in London where the finest bespoke tailors are to be found
- 'whistle and flutes', line 3: suits
- 'thr'penny bits', line 4: tits (breasts); a three penny bit is a pre-decimal coin
- 'mince pies', line 7: eyes
- 'Austin Princess', line 10: a limousine popular with gangsters in the 1960s
- 'Garland', line 12: Judy Garland, an actor and singer
- 'God forbids', line 13: kids
- 'suffragette', line 14: a woman who fought for women to have the vote in early twentieth-century Britain
- 'juniper fumes/of her Vera Lynn', lines 19–20: Vera Lynn means gin, which is made from juniper berries
- 'Emmeline's army', line 20: Emmeline Pankhurst was the leader of the suffragettes
- 'salt/of the earth', lines 22–23: people regarded as the finest of their kind
- 'orchestra stalls', line 30: balls (testicles)
- 'clocking', line 33: noticing, noting
- 'boozers', line 33: not the people who were drinking, but the public houses themselves (a transferred epithet)
- 'Vita and Violet', line 35: Vita Sackville-West and Violet Trefusis, celebrated lesbian lovers
- 'Mile End Road', line 42: the road leading from the City of London to the East End
- 'Protection', line 48: the Kray twins ran a 'protection racket' — local businesses paid regular sums for 'protection' from the Krays' own thugs
- 'dosh', line 49: money
- 'gaff', line 50: premises, place, establishment
- 'bang to rights', line 51: a phrase used by criminals when they felt it was 'a fair cop', i.e. that they had been justly caught by the police; 'banged up' meant put in a cell
- 'butcher's', line 53: look (short for 'butcher's hook, take a look')
- 'Germaine…Diana Dors', lines 55–57: contemporary female icons — Germaine Greer (writer), Brigitte Bardot (actor), Twiggy (model), Lulu (singer), Dusty Springfield (singer), Yoko Ono (artist and wife of John Lennon), Shirley Bassey (singer), Babs (Barbara Windsor, actor friend of the real Kray twins), Sandy Shaw (singer), Diana Dors (actor)
- 'Sinatra', line 64: not Frank but Nancy, his daughter, who became a feminist icon with her song 'These boots are made for walking'

'Elvis's Twin Sister'

Elvis Presley remains an iconic rock and roll figure. Although his decline into self-indulgence, indolence and obesity, and his humiliating death, are widely known, most people prefer to remember his earlier years of glory when he was the leading figure in a revolutionary musical movement. His songs and act were overtly sexual, and yet he remained devoted to his Roman Catholic faith. This poem can be seen as being about both Elvis's imaginary sister and a female version of Elvis — how his talent might have developed had he been born a girl. It is interesting to note that Elvis actually did have a twin, but he was a boy who was stillborn.

This poem is unusual in that it is not a feminist attack. Elvis is hardly referred to, and when he is it is with affection. Duffy makes the persona the twin sister of Elvis to suggest that she is his exact counterpart, and that this is an alternative route that his talents might have taken; a Catholic girl might well choose to join a convent and serve God. There is a suggestion that, although she is clearly content, there are rebellious strands in her character as well, evidenced by the blue suede shoes, and the reference to having 'walked/down Lonely Street', a hint at the events which may have led her to the religious life.

As regards Elvis himself, we learn from the poem that his sister is fond of him, as are the other nuns. When Elvis's twin says 'just like my brother' she confirms that Elvis does at least exist in this poetic world (whereas the female Kray twins *replace* the real-life Kray twins), and is known to the Reverend Mother. Otherwise, apart from the references to the songs, the poem is not about Elvis.

The religious vocation followed by his sister is a reversal of the typical view of Elvis, and there are ironies in a nun who wears blue suede shoes, moves her hips and knows rock songs, but the reader must judge whether there is any real hostility to the situation in which she finds herself or whether she is contented with a fate so much less glorious than her brother's. Duffy probably expects that the reader will know of the unpleasant end to Elvis's life, and realise that his sister is actually better off.

Style and language

Duffy skilfully mimics the style of Tennessee, where Presley was born and brought up, in the American South, e.g. 'y'all', 'Lawdy'. There are several quotations from and references to Elvis's songs; otherwise the style is appropriately casual. There are several pairs of rhyming lines, although not in any regular pattern. The poem is divided into six stanzas of five lines each, some of which contain separate ideas and are end-stopped. Despite the references to Elvis's song's, the poem does not obviously mimic one.

Themes

The theme could be that talent can realise itself in a number of directions or fields. It is not necessary, or necessarily satisfying, to pursue fame and fortune; greater contentment may be found in simple pleasures or even in a religious vocation. It is possible that the quotation from Madonna in the epigraph caused Duffy to investigate just what a female Elvis might have been like.

References and allusions

- '*Are you lonesome tonight? Do you miss me tonight?*': the epigraph quotes the lyrics of Elvis's song 'Are you lonesome tonight?'
- 'convent', line 1: a religious house for women, the equivalent of a monastery; most often, as here, for Roman Catholic women, although other Christian groups have them too
- 'y'all', line 1: 'you all', an expression widely used in the Southern states of the USA
- 'digs', line 9: 1950s slang for appreciates
- 'Gregorian chant', line 11: a form of religious music sung in Latin in monasteries and convents
- '*Pascha nostrum immolatus est...*', line 13: part of a Gregorian chant, literally meaning '[Christ], our Paschal [Easter] lamb, has been sacrificed'
- 'habit', line 14: the simple robes worn by a nun
- 'wimple', line 16: the head-garment worn by nuns to cover their hair
- 'novice-sewn', line 16: sewn by a novice, i.e. a girl or woman in the process of becoming a nun
- 'rosary', line 17: a holy item for Catholics consisting of a set of beads with a cross; a prayer is said for each bead
- 'blue suede shoes', line 20: an unlikely form of footwear for a nun, and a reference to one of Elvis's most famous songs, 'Blue Suede Shoes'
- 'Graceland', line 22: Elvis's house was called Graceland, but this also refers to the Catholic concept of grace, meaning the gift of salvation by God
- 'Lawdy', line 26: originally a contraction of 'praise the lord', but used in the southern states of the USA as a generic exclamation; Elvis recorded a song entitled 'Lawdy Miss Clawdy'
- 'Lonely Street...Heartbreak Hotel', lines 29–30: lyrics from 'Heartbreak Hotel', one of Elvis's most famous songs — 'down at the end of Lonely Street at Heartbreak Hotel'

'Pope Joan'

There is a legend that there was a Pope Joan in the ninth century; for Duffy she is a female counterpart of an archetypally male role. 'Transubstantiation' is the miraculous process by which bread becomes the body of Christ during Mass; 'in nomine patris et filii et spiritus sancti' is Latin for 'in the name of the father, the son and the Holy Ghost'. The poem is shocking because Pope Joan concludes that 'I did not believe a word' and compares the experience of childbirth to religious revelation, calling it a 'miracle'.

'Penelope'

Penelope was the wife of Odysseus, the hero of Homer's *The Odyssey*, an epic poem about Odysseus's journey home after the Trojan War. Penelope sat loyally at home in Ithaca awaiting his return and fighting off suitors. Duffy's Penelope, inevitably, after initially hoping for his return, finds contentment with her pastimes — 'most certainly not waiting' — but he nevertheless returns. She finds that weaving her tapestry, which she began 'to amuse myself', becomes more satisfying than the prospect of the return of her husband.

'Mrs Beast'

This poem can be seen as a feminist manifesto for the collection. Duffy applauds those women who seize the initiative, demand what they need, including sex, and get it on their terms. They have to be, she claims, just as much a 'Beast' as the man to avoid joining the catalogue of female victims, from Eve to Princess Diana. The poem, and the whole collection, is 'words for the lost, the captive beautiful,/the wives, those less fortunate than we'.

'Demeter'

Demeter was the Ancient Greek goddess of fertility. This is a beautiful and lyrical poem about the power of a daughter to bring love and hope to a mother: 'my daughter, my girl, across the fields,/in bare feet, bringing all spring's flowers/to her mother's house.' Duffy assumes that readers will be aware of the bitter irony that Demeter's daughter, Persephone, was subsequently abducted and raped by Hades, the king of the underworld.

Literary terms and concepts

Assessment Objective 1 requires 'insight appropriate to literary study, using appropriate terminology'. The terms below are relevant to the poetry of Carol Ann Duffy and will aid concise argument and precise expression.

allegory	extended metaphor which veils a moral or political underlying meaning
alliteration	repetition of initial letter or sound in adjacent words, e.g. 'a beautiful boy in the bar'
allusion	passing reference to another literary work, without naming it
ambiguity	capacity of words to have two simultaneous meanings in the context as a device for enriching meaning
anachronism	chronological misplacing of person, event or object, e.g. 'Mrs Midas'

analogy	perception of similarity between two things
anecdote	a brief written or spoken account of an amusing incident, often used to illustrate a point
anthropomorphism	attributing human characteristics to an animal or inanimate object
antithesis	contrast of ideas by balancing words or phrases of opposite meaning
archetype	original model used as recurrent symbol
assonance	repetition of vowel sound in words in close proximity, e.g. 'weeps tears'
bathos	sudden change of register from the sublime to the ridiculous
caesura	deliberate break or pause in a line of poetry, signified by punctuation
caricature	exaggerated and ridiculous portrayal of a person built around a specific physical or personality trait, e.g. the pigs in 'Circe'
circumlocution	roundabout way of describing something for rhetorical effect
cliché	predictable and overused expression or situation
climax	moment of intensity to which a series of events has been leading
colloquial	informal language of conversational speech
compound	word made up from two others and hyphenated, e.g. 'stiff-haired'
connotation	association evoked by a word, e.g. 'rosy' suggests warm and healthy
consonance	repetition of consonants in adjacent words
contextuality	historical, social and cultural background of a text
criticism	evaluation of literary text or other artistic work
defamiliarisation	making readers perceive something freshly by using devices which draw attention to themselves or by deviating from ordinary language and conventions
dialect	variety of a language used in a particular area, distinguished by features of grammar and/or vocabulary
dialogue	direct speech of characters engaged in conversation
diction	choice of words; vocabulary from a particular semantic field, e.g. religion
dramatic monologue	lengthy speech, often with accompanying actions, to one or more silent listeners

elegy	lament for the death or permanent loss of someone or something
ellipsis	omission of word(s) for economy or avoidance of repetition
empathy	identifying with a character in a literary work
end-stopped	pause created by punctuation at the end of a line of verse
enjamb(e)ment	run-on line of poetry, usually to reflect its meaning
epigram	short, concise, original and witty saying, often including rhyme, alliteration, assonance or antithesis, e.g. 'Mrs Icarus'
epigraph	inscription at the head of a chapter, poem or book; see 'Weasel Words'
epiphany	sudden and striking revelation of the essence of something sublime
eponymous	main character after whom a work is named, e.g. Penelope
eulogy	speech or writing in praise of someone or something
euphemism	tactful way of referring to something unpleasant or offensive
fable	short fictitious tale conveying a moral, often involving animals or legendary figures; see 'Mrs Aesop'
figurative	using imagery; non-literal use of language
foot/feet	division of syllables into a repeated metrical unit in a line of poetry
form	the way a text is divided and organised; the shape of the text on the page
free verse	poetry without a regular metrical pattern or rhyme
genre	type or form of writing with identifiable characteristics, e.g. epic
half-rhyme	words which almost rhyme, e.g. gape/gap
hyperbole	deliberate exaggeration for effect, e.g. 'I'm so bored I could eat myself'
idiolect	style of speech peculiar to an individual character and recognisable as such
imagery	descriptive language appealing to the senses, usually in the form of simile or metaphor
in medias res	beginning a text in the middle of an event or a conversation
internal rhyme	placement of rhyming words within a line of poetry
intrusive narrator	narrator who addresses the reader or interpolates comments

irony	amusing or cruel reversal of an outcome intended, expected or deserved
juxtaposition	placing side by side for (ironic) contrast
legend	story about historical figure which exaggerates his/her qualities or feats
litotes	expressing an affirmative by the negative of its contrary, e.g. 'not bad' for 'good'
lyrical	expressive of strong feelings, usually love; suggestive of music
metaphor	comparison implied but not stated, and not literally possible, e.g. 'her breasts were a mirror'
metonymy	substituting an attribute for the thing itself
metre	regular series of stressed and unstressed syllables in a line of poetry
monologue	extended speech or thought process by one character
myth	fiction involving supernatural beings which explains natural and social phenomena and embodies traditional and popular ideas
narrative	connected and usually chronological series of events which form a story
neologism	creation of a new word, usually in poetry
onomatopoeia	words which imitate the sound being described, e.g. 'murmuring'
oxymoron	two contradictory terms united in a single phrase
paradox	self-contradictory truth
parody	imitation and exaggeration of style for purpose of humour and ridicule
pathetic fallacy	attributing emotions to objects or natural elements to represent the persona's feelings
pathos	evocation of pity for someone in a situation of suffering and helplessness
periphrasis	expressing something in an unnecessarily lengthy and indirect way
persona	created voice within a text who plays the role of narrator/speaker
personification	human embodiment of an abstraction or object, indicated by the use of a capital letter or she/he
plurality	possible multiple meanings of a text
pun	use of word with double meaning for humorous or enriching effect

reflective	revealing thoughts of writer or character
register	type of expression, level of formality
rhetoric	art of persuasion using emotive language and stylistic devices, e.g. rhetorical questions and exclamations
rhyme	repetition of vowel sounds in words at the end of separate lines of poetry
rhythm	pace and sound pattern of words, created by metre, vowel length, syntax and punctuation
satire	exposing vice or foolishness of a person or institution to ridicule
semantic field	group of words with thematic relationship
semantics	study of influence of words on thought and behaviour
simile	comparison introduced by 'as' or 'like'; epic simile is a lengthy and detailed analogy
sonnet	lyrical poem of 14 lines of rhymed iambic pentameter, usually either Petrarchan or Shakespearean
stanza	another term for a verse; there are various forms depending on the number of lines and type of rhyme scheme
stereotype	category of person with typical characteristics, e.g. a psychopath
stream of consciousness	method used by modernist writers to relate the inmost thoughts and feelings of characters without logical sequence, syntax or (sometimes) punctuation
style	selection and organisation of language elements, related to genre or the individual user of language
surrealism	literary and artistic movement which began in Paris about 1924, typified by the juxtaposition of incongruous ideas or objects in an attempt to express the subconscious free from the controls of reason, as in dreams
symbol	object, person or event which represents something more than itself, e.g. a rose
synecdoche	substitution of the part for the whole, e.g. 'factory hands'
syntax	arrangement of grammar and word order in sentence construction
theme	abstract idea or issue explored in a text
tone	emotional aspect of the voice of a text, e.g. miserable, ecstatic
zeugma	yoking together of two incongruous nouns through their shared grammatical structure

Questions & Answers

Essay questions, specimen plans and examiner notes

The exemplar essay questions that follow can be used for planning practice and/or full essay writing within the time limit, with or without the text. Many have been previously set by different exam boards for various specifications. In each of the four sections there are essay titles with examiners' notes, further questions for practising, and some suggestions for ideas to include in a plan. Two questions are provided with sample student answers. Remember to talk about the poem and the persona, not the poet, and try to hear how the poem would sound if read aloud. The form and the language are essential elements of the poetry, so you must not restrict yourself to a discussion of content.

The question you choose may direct you to one or two prescribed poems or ask you to select your own. Either way you should think about the following:

- Careful selection of poems is crucial to ensure the relevance and success of your essay. The poems you like or are most familiar with are not necessarily the most appropriate for a particular title.
- Show your knowledge of the whole selection as well as your response to and analysis of particular poems.
- Focus closely on the chosen poem(s) but also relate their content and/or language to elsewhere in the selection; link your comments to the overall themes, and suggest ways in which the poem is typical of the poet's work as a whole.
- Do not waste time paraphrasing what happens in a poem; just give a quick summary of its setting and context, along the lines of who is present, where and why.
- Think about reader reaction, using your own as the basis for your response.
- In an open-book exam only include the relevant annotations you have made in the margin and on the text and remember that they need to be organised into a structured response, not just transferred to your essay as a list.

Poem-based questions: prescribed

1 **'The days are mosaic, telling a story for the years/to come' ('Dies Natalis'). Using this poem as your starting-point and by careful examination of at least two other poems, show to what extent you think Duffy's poetry can be said to reflect this 'mosaic'.**

   AO1 Interpretation of 'mosaic' will be key here, with some candidates taking it only to mean a whole made up of disparate pieces, while others will see it as implying a pattern drawn out of an assemblage of apparently unconnected elements.

AO2ii Range of reference is what will distinguish answers here: some candidates will focus simply on narrative, on the stories told, while others will look at the variety of story-tellers and how the different voices in Duffy's poetry build up a composite picture of human experience across time and place.

AO3 What will distinguish candidates here will be the extent to which they examine the varied means Duffy uses to project different characters and attitudes, ranging from isolated diction to register, imagery and overall structure.

AO4 Candidates are required to assess the validity of the view offered of Duffy's poetry, but there is also room for them to suggest a different way of considering her work: breadth of argument will be a significant discriminator here; the quotation hints at the function of poetry, so there is scope too for a wider discussion of this.

AO5ii Reward against this AO will depend on the range of contextual influences candidates explore in response to the prompt in the quotation: answers are likely to vary in scope between the purely historical to the more broadly cultural, covering geographic as well as social and gender influences, considered as significant factors not only in the poetry but also reactions to it.

(Source: Edexcel specimen mark scheme, 2000)

2 **'Duffy is particularly concerned with the gap between appearance and reality.' Starting with 'Model Village', and writing about at least two other poems, discuss this judgement.**

Possible ideas to include in a plan

- appearance/reality is an important theme for Duffy because so many of her characters either have a secret or a fantasy to which they give voice only internally (but Duffy enables us to share it)
- irony/ambiguity of title: physical model village should represent 'model' village but does not
- narrating persona possibly a child – makes naive, stereotypical observations about the model characters she sees
- her naivety is subverted when we hear the inner voices of some village characters – not 'model' at all: they all have a secret
- the poem is a paradox: if this is a (real) model village, then the characters are not real people at all; their voices are merely Duffy's mischievous invention
- narrator suddenly moves from innocence to experience at end of poem – voice fuses with Duffy's
- narrator in 'Psychopath' appears to be a fairground worker, but in reality he is a psycho-pathic murderer – he is an extreme case, because he cannot face up to the reality of what he does
- 'Weasel Words' is about appearance and reality of language: weasel words have the appearance of meaning, but have had reality sucked out; metaphor for the deceit of politicians

- 'Fraud' is another example where appearance is deliberately misleading
- society angle: people (especially in 'Model Village') have to dissemble, to hide their reality, for fear of censure/prejudice/exposure
- ubiquitous image of mirrors reflects the soul – appearance or reality?
- conclusion: this is an important theme for Duffy but by no means the only one

Further questions

3 Remind yourself of 'The Grammar of Light'. Explore the ideas expressed in the poem, and the ways in which they are presented.

4 In 'Standing Female Nude', Duffy writes: 'These artists/take themselves too seriously.' How far do you agree with the opinion that this selection confirms the contrary view that 'poetry can be fun'?

5 By comparing 'Making Money' with a poem of your own choice, discuss Duffy's examination of some preoccupations of the modern age.

6 'Duffy expresses her social criticism by giving voices to characters who reveal their lives as being without purpose.' How far do you agree? You should include in your answer an examination of 'Psychopath', as well as *at least two* other poems of your own choice.

7 'Duffy looks at the reality of our changing world; in her poems she explores what it means to live in an "inclusive" multi-racial society.' Examine 'Comprehensive' and *two or more* poems of your choice in the light of this comment.

8 'Duffy writes powerful poems of loss, betrayal and desire; poems that are personal, but speak to us all about what concerns us as modern readers.' Consider this judgement, using 'Valentine' as a starting point, and writing about *at least two* other poems.

9 Write a detailed critical discussion of 'Dear Norman' and, by referring to a range of her other poems, discuss the extent to which Duffy's voice in this poem is typical of her writing.

Whole-text questions

1 It is sometimes claimed, usually by male critics, that contemporary women poets are only interested in exploring issues related to gender. Does your own detailed reading of the work of Carol Ann Duffy incline you to support or reject that view? Refer closely to at least two poems.

AO1   Candidates will need to offer a definition of 'gender issues'; in some cases this will be limited to sexuality (and sexual orientation), while in others it will encompass social status and attitudes, possibly touching also on philosophical and moral debate.

AO2ii Choice of poems will reflect the extent of candidates' appreciation of the implications of the question; some will not question that the issue of gender is one of Duffy's concerns and will select poems which they take to relate to this issue; others are

likely to consider poems either about gender issues but which transcend these, or those reflecting a variety of concerns.

AO3 What will distinguish candidates here will be the extent to which they examine Duffy's use of poetic form, with some candidates largely ignoring form and taking the content of poems at face value, while others explore the tension she often sets up between form and content both on a small scale, through imagery and tone, and on a large scale, through adoption of a particular genre.

AO4 Breadth of argument will be a significant discriminator here, with some candidates simply responding to the view offered, while others are likely in assessing the validity of the view to consider how Duffy's work might be regarded by other critics of perhaps a different sex, class, age, race.

AO5ii The question clearly focuses on the importance of gender; some candidates may concentrate on biographical detail, asserting rather than demonstrating its relevance; others are likely to consider the effect not only of gender but social, cultural and ethnic influences on Duffy's poetry, critics' views and their own responses alike.

(Source: Edexcel specimen mark scheme, 2000)

2 'All childhood is an emigration.' Choose *three* poems from this collection and explore them in the light of this statement.

Possible ideas to include in a plan

- quotation from 'Originally', one of many poems about people who are alienated, have moved or have lost their roots
- concept important to Duffy because she experienced childhood emigration herself – from Glasgow to Stafford – and was an outsider
- many Duffy personas look back on their childhood with same fondness as migrants look back to their homeland
- categories of emigration/growing up: some fail to make transition; others succeed and look back with nostalgia
- for each of the three selected poems: identify persona and attitude (give linguistic evidence); identify tone from language register, diction; comment on form
- e.g. 'The Good Teachers': persona looks back fondly on a particular year at school (memory triggered by seeing old school photo), reminisces, some resignation, no bitterness
- e.g. 'The Captain of the 1964 *Top of the Form* Team': the persona has completely failed to grow up or escape from his childhood; bitter about failure of his life, reflected in mediocre job, unsatisfactory relationships
- e.g. 'Originally': this immigrant has made the transition successfully, but can still say '*I want our own country*'; the immigrant in 'Foreign' has not been successful
- conclusion: an important general theme for Duffy, treated in a variety of ways

Further questions

3 What interests you about the ways in which Duffy presents thoughts and feelings about love in this collection? Refer to *at least two* poems in your answer.

4 Choose *one* of the poems from *The World's Wife* and discuss it in such a way as to demonstrate what you find interesting and illuminating in its content and form.

5 Discuss Duffy's ability to use her dramatic monologues as an invitation to us, her readers, to sympathise with 'outsiders'.

6 What do you find interesting about the way Duffy presents loving relationships in *three* poems in this collection?

7 Duffy explores through her poetry 'the difficulty and deceptions of contemporary relationships'. How would you evaluate this view of Duffy's poetry? In your answer you should refer to *at least three* poems.

8 To what extent do you agree that in her poetry Duffy explores 'a sense of alienation and a turning away from the past'? You should base your answer on a close examination of *three or more* appropriate poems of your choice.

9 'Duffy specialises in giving voice to the outcast. It is a disturbing but coherent and clearly contemporary voice, that demands our serious attention.' How far do you agree with this judgement? You should refer to *at least three* poems.

10 It has been suggested that Duffy's vocabulary (diction or lexis) is entirely 'unpoetic'. If so, what does she rely on to create her poetic effects? If not, how would you defend her choice of words?

11 A fellow poet has praised Duffy's ability 'to combine the comic and the serious in the same poem'. To what extent does this claim apply to the poems in the selection?

12 A critic has called Duffy 'a ventriloquist poet who speaks in a variety of voices'. To what extent does this claim apply to the poems in the selection?

13 'Throughout her work Duffy demonstrates a fascination with representation, and a key image for her is one of the self who looks in the mirror.' Discuss this comment, referring to *at least three* poems you have studied.

14 Duffy's work has been described as 'darkly comic'. Do you find darkness or comedy predominant in this selection?

15 Choose one poem from *The World's Wife*. By means of a close comparison with one earlier poem, discuss the extent to which you feel Duffy's concerns and techniques have developed.

Poem-based AQA questions on *The World's Wife*

1 Remind yourself of the poem 'Mrs Beast'. To what extent do you agree with the view that, in terms of subject matter and style, this poem is the key to the whole collection?

AQA: characteristics of responses placed in Bands 1–4

(Mark range 1–20; italicised points are those to which the examiners attach the most weight when determining the band in which to place the answer)

AOs 1–3	AO4	
■ Simple narrative of the poem ■ Weak expression ■ *Little or no awareness of Duffy as a poet*	■ *Assertive response*	Band 1 1–6
■ *Accurate account at the surface of the poem* ■ Implicit relevance ■ Adequate expression and basic awareness of style	■ Simple personal response ■ May make *simple or obvious connections with the rest of* The World's Wife	Band 2 7–10
■ *Well-organised exploration of this poem* ■ Secure textual knowledge ■ Clear expression and line of argument	■ Well-informed response which *considers the opinion and offers own ideas* ■ *Thoughtful links to the rest of* The World's Wife	Band 3 11–15
■ *Confident, sophisticated analysis of this poem* ■ Well-structured argument displaying insight and overview	■ *Illuminating consideration of the opinion, making perceptive connections with the rest of* The World's Wife ■ Insight and originality	Band 4 16–20

Examiner's comments

Successful candidates:

- had a secure understanding of 'Mrs Beast'
- were able to connect the poem to others in *The World's Wife* and used it as the starting point for an exploration of the collection's key themes and stylistic features
- focused on the keywords 'To what extent do you agree?' as part of a balanced debate

Less successful candidates:

- were confused by Duffy's use of poetic devices in this poem
- produced simple narratives or paraphrases of the poem
- struggled to make any sort of connection between 'Mrs Beast' and the rest of the collection

2 Remind yourself of the poem 'Queen Kong'. To what extent do you agree with the view that, in terms of subject matter and style, this poem is an exception to the general tone of the collection?

Possible ideas to include in a plan

- typical because a new perspective upon a familiar theme
- 'Queen Kong' is an example of reversal of expectation (i.e. typical of collection) because reader expects giant gorilla to be violent and male, like King Kong
- example of female counterpart, not wife (less common, but several others in collection)
- paradox: she is able to shop in Bloomingdale's therefore fantasy, but King Kong is fantasy anyway, so double fantasy
- she is masterful but tender: causes reader to re-examine prejudices about gorillas — example of a woman in a dominant position, others include 'The Kray Sisters' and 'Circe'
- language is reflective, resigned, grammatical; persona is recollecting fondly in state of tranquillity, in common with a number of other poems in the collection
- differs from other poems in collection because she is not anti-man — she loves him but it is hardly an equal relationship; this is a reversal of the patronising, don't-worry-your-little-head male attitude towards women
- there is no typical style in *The World's Wife*; each persona has her own style to reflect her individual situation and attitude
- conclusion: in important respects 'Queen Kong' is typical of collection, which offers a variety of viewpoints and of reversals of expectation, designed to surprise, and in a wide range of voices and styles, so the approach is predictable but not the outcome — a female who is fond of her man

Further questions

3 Remind yourself of the poem 'Circe'. To what extent do you agree with the view that, in terms of subject matter and style, this poem is typical of the whole collection?

4 Remind yourself of the poem 'Little Red-Cap'. To what extent do you agree with the view that, in terms of subject matter and style, this poem is a fitting introduction to the whole collection?

Whole-text AQA questions on *The World's Wife*

1 '*The World's Wife* is a feminist manifesto.' To what extent do you agree with this judgement? In your answer, you should *either* refer to *two* or *three* poems in detail *or* range more widely through the collection.

AQA: characteristics of responses placed in Bands 1–4

(Mark range 1–20; italicised points are those to which the examiners attach the most weight when determining the band in which to place the answer)

AOs 1–3	AO4	
■ Narrative or paraphrase ■ Poor expression ■ *Little or no awareness of Duffy's poetic technique*	■ Struggles to engage with keywords ■ Assertion	Band 1 1–6
■ *Sensible choice of poems, displaying basic engagement with the question* ■ Adequate expression ■ *Some awareness of Duffy's style*	■ *Understands opinion and states a simple personal response* ■ May offer some obviously contrasting examples	Band 2 7–10
■ Shaped and coherent response ■ *Secure knowledge of* The World's Wife; *thoughtful analysis of Duffy's technique*	■ *Balanced consideration of opinion,* offering both support and alternatives ■ Well-informed, personal response	Band 3 11–15
■ Confident, sophisticated analysis of the poetry ■ Well-structured argument displaying insight and overview	■ Mature and perceptive response to opinion ■ *Overview of* The World's Wife enables candidate to reach well-informed, independent conclusion	Band 4 16–20

Examiner's comments

Successful candidates:

- were able to explore Duffy's variety of voices
- understood that Duffy employs this technique in different ways and to different effects
- answered the question of 'To what extent do you agree?' by developing a balanced debate which applied the keyword 'feminist' to a variety of poems

Less successful candidates:

- wrote simple accounts of two poems but ignored the question of 'To what extent do you agree?'
- simply agreed with the given view and did not offer any alternatives or counter-arguments
- struggled to engage with the keyword 'feminist'

2 'Subversion of reader expectation is the predominant feature of *The World's Wife*.'
Do you agree with this judgement? In your answer, you should *either* refer to *two*
or *three* poems in detail *or* range more widely through the collection.

Possible ideas to include in a plan

- Duffy makes no concessions to her readers, and their expectations can only be
  subverted if they have them. Assuming that readers know enough about the original
  characters, then in very many cases *The World's Wife* poems aim to subvert them —
  most of the humour and the pleasure in the poems lies in Duffy subverting cultural icons
  and our getting the joke.
- 'Penelope': Penelope's faithful waiting for Odysseus, fending off suitors, is a strong icon
  of female submission, subverted by Duffy: Penelope finds she has the opportunity to
  develop her own interests and does not need Odysseus. Tone confident, not angry or
  bitter.
- 'The Kray Sisters': female equivalent of notorious murdering gangsters would be
  expected to be violent. They do have the swaggering confidence but use their power
  to benefit other women, not to harm people. Cockney rhyming slang style is appropriate.
- 'Little Red-Cap': about a young girl being seduced by a predatory man, 'the wolf'. But
  this is her choice and doing, her deliberate attempt to use him to escape from childhood,
  and when she is satisfied she axes him. Confident, proud retrospective monologue;
  many language subtleties.
- Yes, this is one of the central concerns of *The World's Wife*; it is hard to find exceptions,
  but they function in a range of ways. It is, however, not the only concern: feminism,
  revenge and the offering of a new perspective on well-known historical characters are
  also important.

Further questions

3 'Duffy's treatment of Greek mythological themes in *The World's Wife* is part of a
project to construct an alternative feminist mythology.' Do you agree with this
judgement? In your answer, you should *either* refer to *two* or *three* poems in detail
or range more widely through the collection.

4 'Duffy's mistreated and angry women in *The World's Wife* are just as stereotyped
as the men who abuse them.' Do you agree with this judgement? In your answer,
you should *either* refer to *two* or *three* poems in detail *or* range more widely
through the collection.

Sample essays

Below are two essays of different types, both falling within the top band. You can judge them against the Assessment Objectives for this text for your exam board and decide on the mark you think each deserves and why. You will be able to see ways in which each could be improved in terms of content, style and accuracy.

Sample essay 1: poem-based

'In her poetry Carol Ann Duffy is particularly concerned to portray individuals who are viewed as social outcasts; she wants the reader to understand rather than to judge.' Consider this judgement, referring to 'Psychopath' and at least two other poems.

Carol Ann Duffy's poetry covers a wide cross-section of characters from most groups in society, varying in age, race, gender and background. A significant number of her poems present people who are poorly adjusted, inadequate, or simply different from those around them. Although readers are likely to be able to relate to many of the personas she portrays, some will be less familiar and can even be shocking for a reader.

A society should be inclusive, able to accommodate those who feel lonely or isolated, or those who differ from the norm in some way, but too often such people are discriminated against or treated as social outcasts. Fairground workers are itinerants and are often treated like 'travellers', who are similarly ostracised and viewed as beyond the law. Duffy's own childhood experiences as an 'outsider' in Stafford may have contributed to her concern for people in such situations. Such personas are often forced to hide their deepest secrets under a cloak of 'normality'. Appearance and reality are therefore major themes investigated by Duffy in her poetry.

The eponymous persona of the poem 'Psychopath' is a striking example of all these ideas. Although an extreme personality – a remorseless psychopathic killer – he appears to fit in with the other workers in the fair. He is able to do this because his violent acts seem to have no effect upon him: readers are deeply shocked when they see the ease with which the 'Psychopath' can detach himself from his actions and their consequences. 'She is in the canal', he says, with absolute indifference, of the young girl he has raped and casually killed.

We first see the persona combing his hair and admiring himself in a mirror, ready to move on from the events of the evening. 'Tomorrow will find me somewhere else, with a loss of memory', he says. He then recounts the events of the evening, in a wholly emotionless way, but Duffy's attitude to him is not simple: she lets the reader glimpse two sexually damaging events in his childhood ('Dirty Alice' who 'flicked [his] dick out' and 'jeered' at it, and his mother with the 'Rent Man'). Duffy also, in a device she often employs, lends the semi-literate youth a voice which cannot be his own, when he waxes lyrical: '...as if the town has held its breath/to watch the Wheel go round above the dreary homes.' Duffy is

also, in passing, satirising the dreariness of ordinary life which makes funfairs necessary to relieve the tedium. There is also a hint, at the end of the poem, that the psychopath, for all his bravado ('I could be anything', he says; 'Deep down I'm talented'), is aware that there may be consequences when he mentions Ruth Ellis, a notorious murderer who had recently been hanged, and the ambiguity of the barman calling 'time' as if his time were up.

Overall, Duffy's presentation of a character who would normally be seen as repugnant, although it pulls no punches, does invite the reader to ask about the circumstances which caused the youth to be like this, and to ask whether there might be some sensitivity or potential buried somewhere within.

'Model Village' is another poem which deals with characters who have something to hide, and would certainly be social outcasts to a greater or lesser degree if their innermost secrets were to be known. Miss Maiden, seemingly an 'old maid', has actually killed her own mother after she blocked her attempts to find a lover; the nervous Farmer is 'digging, desperately' for something after having an unnerving experience; and the Vicar is fixated in childhood. 'I am naughty', he says (privately); his sadomasochistic fantasies make him 'tremble and dissolve into childhood'. Duffy's approach here is mischievous: the narrator of the poem is possibly a naive child visiting a model village, and Duffy puts words into the mouths of the model humans – who reveal that they are hardly 'model' citizens at all. But this seems somewhat different from the more 'real' characters she presents elsewhere, even if they no doubt reflect real people. The child narrator becomes knowing during the course of the poem, as if the urgent burden of the unspoken secrets of the characters has communicated itself to her. The final inhabitant of the village is a Duffy-like Librarian whose secret is that she knows the secrets of all the others: 'Behind each front door lurks truth, danger', she says (note the key juxtaposition of 'truth' and 'danger', a fact for many Duffy characters).

A different kind of social outcast is presented in 'Selling Manhattan', the title poem of Duffy's second collection. The poem deals with the ways in which the female Native American persona has been suppressed by the forces of European colonisation repre-sented by the persona of the epigraph: '*Now get your red ass out of here.*' The European achieves his cynical, materialist aims by 'brandish[ing]/fire-arms and fire-water'. Duffy gives the woman a voice, and by allowing us to hear her thoughts the reader is immediately made aware of the moral superiority of the downtrodden natives. 'Today I can hear again and plainly see', she sees: 'No good will come of this.' She foresees the corruption of the sacred land by the white man: 'I wonder if the spirit of the water has anything/to say. That you will poison it.' Her man has been killed by the invaders, but she has come to terms with it with the wisdom of her people: 'Loss holds the silence of great stones.' And although her days are numbered, she has confidence in the beliefs she holds: 'I will live in the ghost of the grasshopper and buffalo.' Although marginalised by the colonists, Duffy offers the reader the opportunity to view the struggle from a very different perspective.

Another group of social outcasts with whom Duffy has particular sympathy is those subjected to racial discrimination. The immigrant persona in 'Foreign' feels alone and hated where she lives, having to see a name for herself 'sprayed in red/against a brick wall. A hate name. Red like blood'. She feels 'inarticulate, because this is not home'. Duffy directly invites the reader to empathise with the persona by the bold opening of the poem: 'Imagine living in a strange, dark city for twenty years.'

Duffy's role is to give a voice to all these marginalised people and hence to make it possible for the reader to gain a glimpse of their worlds, their secret lives and fears, their hopes. In the process, she as poet often lends otherwise inarticulate people a little assistance in the formulation of thoughts which, in many cases, they have never spoken aloud. She undoubtedly helps the reader to understand; it is the up to the reader whether, and how, they judge. The 'Psychopath' rather perceptively says: 'You get one chance in this life/and if you screw it you're done for.'

Sample essay 2: whole-text

Does Carol Ann Duffy use her poems to criticise aspects of society?

It is characteristic of Carol Ann Duffy's poetry that she depicts individuals and situations and allows them to speak for themselves. She never preaches, and indeed rarely adopts a personal position; rather, by subtle nuancing, she guides the reader towards a position in sympathy with her own. She rarely actually criticises anything; but implicit in much of her poetry is a sharp social criticism of existing arrangements and the price exacted for them from many members of society.

A good example is 'Education for Leisure'. This poem has clear affinities with 'Psychopath', in that both portray inadequate young men with a taste (in varying degrees) for violence. The title is ironic: it was indeed a goal of the mass education movement after 1944 that all citizens should be educated to make constructive use of their leisure time; but not that they should be content with a life of purposeless idleness on the dole. The poem is an internal monologue delivered by a young man who has recently left school but has not found work (there is no evidence he has even tried). Bored out of his mind (compare the persona of 'Stealing': 'Mostly I'm so bored I could eat myself'), he imagines himself a god and kills flies and a goldfish as an exercise in power. The poem becomes chilling at the end when, having begun by saying 'Today I am going to kill something', the persona takes the kitchen knife and, addressing the reader directly, says 'I touch your arm'. In this, as in so many of her portraits, Duffy gives a hint of an alternative that might have been, when the persona quotes Shakespeare (albeit to justify his murderous purposes). The persona did receive an education, and yet is unemployed and has no future. We are given no information as to why this is; the reader must infer or guess, but while the implied criticism of a society which allows this to happen is clear enough, it is left to the reader to draw this interpretation.

'Standing Female Nude' is the title-poem of Duffy's first collection and it touches upon a number of themes central to her work. The persona is the model for Georges Braque as he paints his famous Cubist work of the same name, and in Duffy's hands she is a strong,

independent woman. The social criticism is powerful: in turn-of-the-century Paris, both artist and model bemoan the situation where they have to prostitute their talents for rich, bourgeois patrons. Although the artist-model relationship is often seen as exploitative (he wears clothes, she is naked; he pays her to display her body) Duffy shows that they are, in different ways, both victims ('I ask him Why do you do this? Because/I have to'). The economic imperatives which drive the model to stand naked, 'Belly nipple arse in the window light', are clear enough: 'He is concerned with light, space./I with the next meal.' And the source of the money for the next meal: 'The bourgeoisie will coo/at such an image of a river-whore'. The persona summarises: 'Both poor, we make our living how we can.'

A very different kind of criticism of society informs the poem 'The Dolphins'. The persona here is a dolphin, captured by humans and made to perform for other humans. The pathos of the trapped, doomed creature evokes powerful responses in the reader. 'We are in our element but we are not free', the dolphin-persona comments. 'We have found no truth in these waters...We were blessed and now we are not blessed.' Duffy, as always, does not comment directly, but leaves the reader to ask why it is permitted for dolphins to be treated in this way. 'There is no hope...There is a man and our mind knows we will die here.'

It is interesting that all of these poems are from *Standing Female Nude*, Duffy's most politically-engaged collection, as is 'A Healthy Meal', another poem which clearly criticises an aspect of society − in this case wealthy, pretentious 'gourmets' who are indifferent to the suffering inflicted upon animals by their tastes. Unusually, the voice is that of Duffy herself; there is no mediating persona, and the attack is the more vicious as a consequence. But the points are subtly made: 'The menu/lists the recent dead in French' − which surprises, because animals are not usually referred to as 'the dead', a phrase generally reserved for humans. 'There are...sauces to gag the groans of abattoirs.' Duffy's attack is equally upon the greedy, insensitive people involved ('The woman chewing suckling pig/must sleep with her husband later', implying there is little difference between the pigs and the man) and a society that tolerates such cruelty.

There is no doubt that Duffy feels passionately about a number of aspects of British society, perhaps not surprising for the daughter of a Labour party worker who experienced discrimination as an outsider in her youth. Although her attacks are always indirect, they are arguably more effective for being placed in the mouth and voice of a persona, leaving the reader to draw the desired conclusion. Of course, there are many other issues which Duffy speaks of in her poetry − relations between men and women, and between women and women, most obviously − but social criticism is an important part of her poetic work.

Further study

Relatively little has been published in book form about the poetry of Carol Ann Duffy, despite its popularity and regular appearance on A-level specifications. However, *Carol Ann Duffy* (2001) by Deryn Rees-Jones, part of Northcote House Educational Publishers' *Writers and Their Work* series, discusses Duffy's first four collections, although it does not include *The World's Wife*.

The majority of the criticism available is, appropriately for such a contemporary voice, to be found on the internet. The 'Knitting Circle' from South Bank University has a useful bibliography at **http://myweb.lsbu.ac.uk/~stafflag/carol annduffy.html**. Steve Brown's site at **http://www.stevebrown.clara.net/html/ carol_ann_duffy.htm** includes commentaries on all the poems in the *Mean Time* collection. You can find a list of general links at **http://www.geocities.com/klf67/ dlinks.html**.

For *The World's Wife*, there is an entertaining PowerPoint presentation at **http://www.thelearningbank.co.uk/shireland/subjects/english/assets/docs/carol annduffy.ppt** which is an AS revision exercise specifically on the collection. A detailed review of *The World's Wife* can be found **at http://www.poetrymagazines.org.uk/ magazine/record.asp?id=4292**.

A Google search on 'Carol Ann Duffy' returns tens of thousands of pages, so there may well be other useful resources out there on the fast-changing worldwide web.